Mastering Prezi for Presentations

Engage your audience visually with stunning Prezi presentation designs and be the envy of your colleagues who use PowerPoint

Russell Anderson-Williams

BIRMINGHAM - MUMBAI

Mastering Prezi for Business Presentations

First published: July 2012

Production Reference: 1170712

Published by Packt Publishing Ltd.
Livery Place
35 Livery Street
Birmingham B3 2PB, UK.

ISBN 978-1-84969-302-8

www.packtpub.com

Cover Image by John M. Quick (john.m.quick@gmail.com)

Credits

Author

Russell Anderson-Williams

Reviewers

Ned Potter

Mikah J. Pritchard

Acquisition Editor

Usha Iyer

Lead Technical Editor

Pramila Balan

Technical Editor

Vrinda Amberkar

Project Coordinator

Michelle Quadros

Proofreader

Lynda Sliwoski

Indexer

Hemangini Bari

Graphics

Valentina D'Silva

Manu Joseph

Production Coordinator

Prachali Bhiwandkar

Cover Work

Prachali Bhiwandkar

About the Author

Russell Anderson-Williams is the founder of www.theprezenter.com, which is dedicated to educating Prezi users in best practice, sharing advice, tips in design, and more than anything, changing the mindset of Prezi users to that of a non-linear thinker. A creative and visual thinker, Russell has a strong background in visual communication and graphic design, as well as a long career in training and education. Russell has designed and delivered hundreds of visually stimulating training presentations for some of the world's biggest companies in a variety of sectors. By merging his love and passion for educating people with his joy for all things wonderfully visual he has set a course to turn anyone in the business world into a Prezi master through his onsite training programs, and tirelessly blogging about everything Prezi related. He resides in the extremely creative city of Bristol in the United Kingdom where he works in training design, Prezi design and training, and anything else that allows his creativity to run wild.

Acknowledgement

I'd like to thank Packt Publishing for their support and guidance in what at first seemed like a huge challenge. They made it a very easy journey, so thanks to one and all.

I also want to thank the team at Prezi, Peter Arvai (Founder, CEO), Adam Somlai-Fischer (Founder, Head of Design), Drew Banks (Head of Marketing), and Zoli Radnai (Community Manager), for your support and appreciation of what I'm trying to do. The same goes for every single Prezi employee who works tirelessly to bring the world an incredible product. You guys really are going to change the world by making information more engaging and easier to digest. Thank you!

My biggest thanks has to go out to my wife Natalie (a self-confessed non-creative) for having the patience to put up with my crazy creative ramblings that probably made no sense to her at all. Thank you darling for always taking the time to listen and also keeping me grounded when I get a little too carried away with my ideas. You're the best.

About the Reviewers

Ned Potter is an Academic Librarian in the UK, at the University of York. As an information professional he has won various awards, including being named a Mover & Shaker by Library Journal in the "Marketing" category. He is the author of *Library Marketing Toolkit*, published in 2012.

Ned teaches at classes, and presents and writes on emerging technologies and marketing. He is a member of the Prezi Pioneer program and has produced extremely popular online guides to the platform, endorsed and promoted by Prezi themselves. He can be found online at www.thewikiman.org, or you can access his Prezi page via http://bit.ly/howtoprezi.

Mikah Pritchard holds a B.S. in Psychology from Oakland City University. She is currently pursuing M.S. Ed. in Instructional Systems Technology at Indiana University. She has had an interest in Educational Psychology and Education Studies throughout her academic and professional career, which has involved the work in graphic design, online instructional materials, and non-traditional student education, including adult learners. Combining her passions of technology and educational psychology in her current position, Mikah works as an Instructional Technologist at DePauw University.

www.PacktPub.com

Support files, eBooks, discount offers and more

You might want to visit www.PacktPub.com for support files and downloads related to your book.

Did you know that Packt offers eBook versions of every book published, with PDF and ePub files available? You can upgrade to the eBook version at www.PacktPub.com and as a print book customer, you are entitled to a discount on the eBook copy. Get in touch with us at service@packtpub.com for more details.

At www.PacktPub.com, you can also read a collection of free technical articles, sign up for a range of free newsletters and receive exclusive discounts and offers on Packt books and eBooks.

http://PacktLib.PacktPub.com

Do you need instant solutions to your IT questions? PacktLib is Packt's online digital book library. Here, you can access, read and search across Packt's entire library of books.

Why Subscribe?

- Fully searchable across every book published by Packt
- Copy and paste, print and bookmark content
- On demand and accessible via web browser

Free Access for Packt account holders

If you have an account with Packt at www.PacktPub.com, you can use this to access PacktLib today and view nine entirely free books. Simply use your login credentials for immediate access.

This book is dedicated to anyone in business who fights every day to inject a little more creativity into their world. For anyone who's sat through hundreds of hours of tireless slides over the last few decades and wants something new. For everyone in business who understands that it's not always what you say, but how you say it. This book is for all of you. Keep fighting the good fight and never do anything just because that's how it's always been done!

- Russell Anderson-Williams

Table of Contents

Preface

If you've discovered Prezi in the last few years or even very recently, you have joined part of an interesting movement that's rapidly changing how ideas are shared. If you're reading this now then there's no doubt in our minds you're completely sold on the fact that business presentations need to change. You're probably also sold on the fact that Prezi is exactly what's needed to make that change. In this book you'll find all the tools and guidance to take your business presentations to the next level, and build on what you already know about Prezi. Our aim is to take you from Prezi user to Prezi master, and we hope you enjoy the ride.

What this book covers

Chapter 1, *Best Practices with Imagery*, will show two different types of imagery. It will help you understand the pros and cons of using either within the Prezi canvas. There are also useful tips on where to find imagery for your Prezi designs and how to create some of your own.

Chapter 2, *Using Audio*, teaches you how to add audio to your canvas and understand when this technique should and shouldn't be used. Audio can bring a whole new dimension to your Prezi designs. It will also make your Prezi very engaging for anyone viewing it online.

Chapter 3, *Inserting a Video*, explores the benefits of using video files that are stored offline or online. We will also look at how to create your own YouTube account to edit and manage your online video files.

Chapter 4, *Approaching Your Prezi Design*, will help you understand the most logical and time-saving way to approach your Prezi design. You'll see exactly why Mind Mapping and planning your Prezis are so important, and you'll also learn the three Prezi design steps to help you build perfect Prezis every time.

Chapter 5, Projecting Your Prezi, gives you some simple facts about projectors that you probably never knew before. With this new knowledge you'll understand why some of your Prezi designs don't look the same once projected onto a big screen. This is an extremely useful chapter that will help keep each and every frame of your Prezi design looking great.

Chapter 6, Prezis for Online Delivery, gives you some simple tips to help engage with your audience and keep them focused when exploring a Prezi on their own. Some of your Prezis will be accessed by colleagues and customers online. Because of this you'll need to take a slightly different approach and think about your audience a lot more.

Chapter 7, Importing Slides into Prezi, helps you understand the Insert PPT feature, and also gives great tips on how to truly turn linear slides into non-linear presentations. With PowerPoint being so dominant in business presentations for such a long time there's no doubt you'll need to Prezify slides for your organization.

Chapter 8, Prezi for iPad and Android, explains how to use the Prezi viewer for iPad, and also gives great advice on how to present using a tablet device. If you use an iPad or Android tablet for business, then why not use it to present new ideas to your colleagues and managers at work?

Chapter 9, Mastering the Newer Prezi Features, will help you master some of the newest Prezi features available as the Prezi software is improving all the time. In this chapter, you will learn how to make the most out of templates, customize shapes, group objects together, and much more.

Chapter 10, Prezi Meeting, will enable you and your colleagues to share ideas in an exciting and engaging way using Prezi Meeting. There are lots of step-by-step instructions on how to set up a meeting, and also useful tips to make sure the meetings you host stay focused and have meaning.

Chapter 11, Getting Prezi through the Door, explores some of the barriers you may face when introducing Prezi to your business. This is going to be just as hard as mastering the tool itself, but we've given you lots of useful tips to help get Prezi through the door and into the hands of your colleagues.

What you need for this book

So long as you've used the Prezi software to build at least one presentation, and have a basic understanding and appreciation of what it can do, you'll be able to benefit from this book.

Who this book is for

This book is for anyone in business that already uses Prezi and wants to take their skills to the next level. Even if you have only just grasped the basics of Prezi, this book will help you think, plan, approach, and build Prezis that engage and inspire your colleagues and customers like never before.

Conventions

In this book, you will find a number of styles of text that distinguish between different kinds of information. Here are some examples of these styles, and an explanation of their meaning.

Code words in text are shown as follows: "This will save your movie as a Windows Media Video (.wmv) file."

New terms and **important words** are shown in bold. Words that you see on the screen, in menus or dialog boxes for example, appear in the text like this: "Always click on the **Advanced Image Search** option to the right of the screen and fine-tune your search before selecting an image."

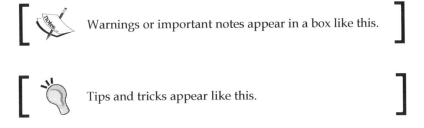

Warnings or important notes appear in a box like this.

Tips and tricks appear like this.

Reader feedback

Feedback from our readers is always welcome. Let us know what you think about this book—what you liked or may have disliked. Reader feedback is important for us to develop titles that you really get the most out of.

To send us general feedback, simply send an e-mail to feedback@packtpub.com, and mention the book title through the subject of your message.

If there is a topic that you have expertise in and you are interested in either writing or contributing to a book, see our author guide on www.packtpub.com/authors.

Customer support

Now that you are the proud owner of a Packt book, we have a number of things to help you to get the most from your purchase.

Errata

Although we have taken every care to ensure the accuracy of our content, mistakes do happen. If you find a mistake in one of our books—maybe a mistake in the text or the code—we would be grateful if you would report this to us. By doing so, you can save other readers from frustration and help us improve subsequent versions of this book. If you find any errata, please report them by visiting `http://www.packtpub.com/support`, selecting your book, clicking on the **errata submission form** link, and entering the details of your errata. Once your errata are verified, your submission will be accepted and the errata will be uploaded to our website, or added to any list of existing errata, under the Errata section of that title.

Piracy

Piracy of copyright material on the Internet is an ongoing problem across all media. At Packt, we take the protection of our copyright and licenses very seriously. If you come across any illegal copies of our works, in any form, on the Internet, please provide us with the location address or website name immediately so that we can pursue a remedy.

Please contact us at `copyright@packtpub.com` with a link to the suspected pirated material.

We appreciate your help in protecting our authors, and our ability to bring you valuable content.

Questions

You can contact us at `questions@packtpub.com` if you are having a problem with any aspect of the book, and we will do our best to address it.

Best Practices with Imagery

First and foremost, Prezi is a tool for storytelling. If an image really can say a thousand words, then it's crucial that you use the right kind of imagery in Prezi to deliver your message in the most powerful way possible.

In this chapter we will explore two different kinds of imagery, and look at how Prezi copes with each. You'll also get some advanced tips on how to create your own imagery that works well with Prezi. By the end of the chapter you will understand the benefits of using certain types of imagery within your Prezi, and be well on the way to mastering this element of your Prezi designs. In this chapter, we cover:

- What raster and vector images are
- Benefits of raster and vector images in your Prezi
- Places to find great imagery
- How to create your own vector imagery
- Creating illustrations for Prezi

Raster and vector images

You may not have come across the terms raster and vector before but they are used to describe two different types of imagery. If you've been building presentations for a while in Prezi or another piece of software, the chances are you've scanned through hundreds and hundreds of raster and vector images without even realizing it. After all, why would you need to know these terms? All you need is to make great presentations for your business, right?

While we totally agree that you don't need to be a professor of the arts to build great presentations, we do believe that knowing the difference between your raster and vector imagery will benefit you massively and help you become a true master of Prezi.

We hope you'll agree that the best Prezis are always the ones that have obviously been planned very well from the start. If you're a reader of my blog, then you'll know that I love to preach about the importance of planning before you even touch the Prezi software. A part of that early planning should be deciding what type of imagery you're going to use, and if there is a particular style you want your Prezi to have. You might also want your Prezi to be small in file size, which is another reason why choosing the right imagery will help.

Let's explore raster and vector imagery together and you can make up your own mind as to which would be right for you and your Prezis.

What are raster images?

A raster image is simply an image made up of tiny pixels of color. Depending on the size of the image there will be hundreds, or even thousands of different pixels placed together in the right way to form the image you see.

In the following raster image, you can see that at normal size it looks great, and there is lots of different shading. However, the right-hand side shows that when you zoom into this image using Prezi, you will start to see the individual pixels that make up the shaded areas. This degrades the quality of the image when viewed at this size.

The preceding image has been saved as a **PNG (Portable Network Graphics)** file using the much loved Adobe Photoshop.

Some other raster graphics editors you could use to create raster images are:

- KolourPaint
- GIMP
- GrafX2

All of the preceding raster graphics editors have their own advantages over one another, so I'd recommend you take 15 minutes out of your day to research them and see which one you would prefer.

Raster file formats

I mentioned that the example image shown previously was saved as a PNG file which is one of the formats Prezi will accept through the insert image menu option. You probably know already that Prezi will also accept **JPEG (Joint Photographic Experts Group)**, **GIF (Graphics Interchange Format)**, and, **PDF (Portable Document Format)** images, "but what do these different files mean?" I hear you shout!

Raster formats within Prezi

File format	Uses	Tips
.jpeg	Uses 16 million colors, so it is perfect for photographs and images with lots of shading.	Compression can be adjusted so you decide the trade-off between image size and quality.
.gif	Great at compressing images that have large blocks of the same color, that is, logos or shapes. Also supports transparency.	Avoid using this format for photographs and images with shading.
.png	Has many of the same qualities as .gif but compresses images in a much better way.	Supports transparency which is extremely useful in Prezi when overlaying images.
.pdf	This format preserves all visual elements within the file and compresses the file size very effectively. This format is useful when importing PowerPoint slides. This is discussed later in *Chapter 7, Importing Slides into Prezi*.	Prezi desktop player will need to convert the PDF files so an Internet connection is needed for this.

What are vector images?

Vector images are not made up of pixels like raster images, but instead they are created using points, lines, curves, and shapes to represent a computer graphic. They use mathematical functions to determine where everything sits in the image.

All of this sounds very technical, doesn't it? Here's what you really need to know about vector images to determine whether or not you'll use them in your Prezis.

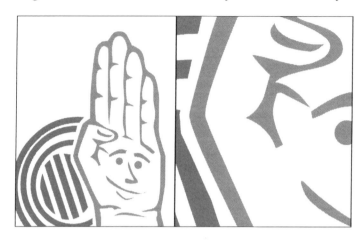

The preceding image has been created in Adobe Illustrator and saved as a PDF file. You can clearly see in the zoomed section on the right that there is absolutely no loss of image quality. I'll come back to this point later, but hopefully you've just had one of those nice "ahah" moments!

You can probably tell by now that I'm a big fan of Adobe products, but I do appreciate that there are other (less expensive) pieces of software for working with vector images. Here are a few you should look into:

- Inkscape
- DrawIt (Mac format only)
- DrawPlus

 Later in this chapter, I'll show you how to create your own vector images using Inkscape. Keep reading though because there's more you need to know before you get to that stage.

Vector file formats

Vector graphic editors like the ones mentioned previously will allow you to export your images in many different file types. The only ones that matter to us though are PDF and **SWF (Small Web Format)** because these are the only two file types that can handle vector images and are supported by Prezi. The following table gives a quick explanation of each file format along with some tips on using them in Prezi.

Vector formats within Prezi

File format	Uses	Tips
.pdf	This format preserves all visual elements within the file and compresses the file size very effectively.	Prezi desktop player will need to convert .pdf files, so, an Internet connection is needed for this.
.swf	Very fast loading format with excellent compression for small file size. Also supports animation (if you know how!)	Supports transparency like .png and .gif files, so, is very useful in Prezi.

 I should state that PDF is not strictly a vector file format, but exporting vector images to this format preserves the image details for inserting into Prezi. This means that you won't get any pixilation like that of a raster image.

What are the benefits of Prezi?

I hope you're now starting to understand the roles that these two very important image types play in getting your Prezi looking great and loading fast.

This book is all about you mastering Prezi, so, it's vital that you understand the impact that everything explained so far has on your Prezi designs.

Imagery Types	Benefits in Prezi	Drawbacks in Prezi
Raster (.jpg, .gif, .png)	There are literally thousands of imagery types available to you online so with some patience you should be able to find some great imagery for your Prezi. Most raster images will be photographs which give more life to your Prezi. Zooming in and out of detail is very effective when using raster images saved at a high resolution. You can use Prezis built-in Google search to quickly find raster images.	It's difficult to find lots of raster imagery in the same consistent style unless you pay for it from an online library. Zooming in too close to raster imagery will cause pixilation in Prezi. Big raster images can be slow to load when users first open a Prezi. Lots of raster images in Prezi will mean a larger file size for your presentation.

Imagery Types	Benefits in Prezi	Drawbacks in Prezi
Vector (.swf, .pdf)	Vector images will always have good compression so file size is extremely small.	Quality vector images will not show up in the Prezi image search feature detailed.
	You'll be able to zoom into a vector image without any loss of quality or pixilation.	Vector images do not look like real life photographs, and this can sometimes be a distraction to anyone viewing your Prezi.
	Vector images are scalable so enlarging them will not affect the quality of the image at all.	
	It is possible to take a raster image and "vectorise" it to get all of the benefits mentioned previously.	

 I am hoping that by now you have started to understand the benefits listed previously, and may be in favor of either raster or vector. If not, then keep on reading and I'm sure you'll come to a conclusion very soon.

Where can you find great imagery?

One thing we all struggle with when creating presentations is finding the right image to deliver our message. You know exactly what you want to say, and if you could just find the right image to accompany your words, then your whole presentation will have a much bigger impact on its audience.

The problem is, of course, that we all have tight (and usually unrealistic) deadlines to meet, and we are probably trying to work on several different projects at once. There isn't enough time in the day to spend it looking at images, but you do want your Prezi to look great.

Following are a few ways of finding the right images, starting with the least time-consuming methods. If you live on some strange planet other than earth, and have the luxury of time to seek out the perfect images, then you'll definitely want to take a look at the latter half of this section. For the rest of us earthlings to whom time is precious, I'm sure you'll find some useful tips at the start.

Prezi Insert from web

The most time-efficient method for finding imagery is, without a doubt, by starting in Prezi itself and using the "insert image from web" function.

To access this, click on **INSERT** from the Prezi menu, then click on **IMAGE** to open the **Insert image** dialogue box, as shown in the following screenshot:

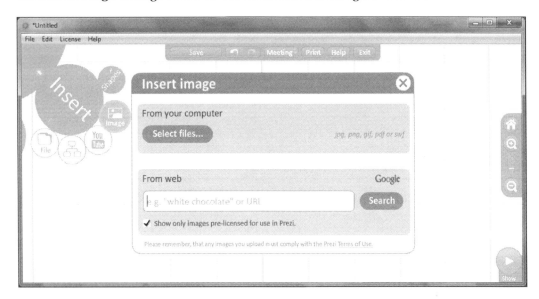

There are two parts to the **Insert image** dialogue box, but as we're focusing on the least time-consuming method for finding and inserting new imagery, let's look at the bottom part titled **From web**.

The **From web** feature allows you to run a Google image search by entering a keyword or phrase into the search panel.

> **Pre-licensed images tick box**
>
> The tick box marked **Show only images pre-licensed for use in Prezi** should remain ticked. Removing it will allow copyrighted images to appear in your search. These images cannot be used unless you gain permission from the image owner – usually at a cost!

Enter the word **Chocolate** into the search box and click on the **SEARCH** button. You'll then see a series of images linked to that keyword which you can scroll through and select as shown in the following screenshot:

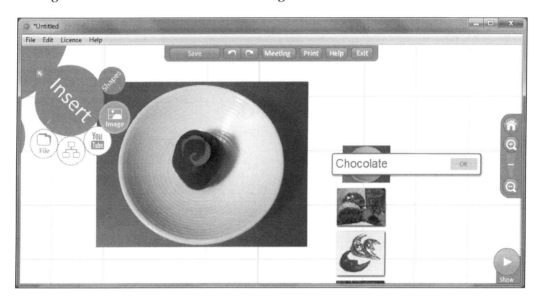

The zoom test

If you see an image that you like, then select it but don't click on the **OK** button just yet. Before you fully insert it into your Prezi, move over to the left of the Prezi screen and use the zoom button to take a closer look at the image. If you zoom in a little and the image starts to lose quality and is pixilated, then it has probably been saved at a very low resolution.

Always zoom in and check the quality of the image first, especially if you know you're going to zoom into it at some stage in your Prezi.

Limitations of the Insert From web function

There's no doubt that using the **Insert From web** function is the fastest way to find images for your Prezi, but it does have its limitations. Here are some things you won't be able to do:

- Check the image dimensions, that is, width and height in pixels
- See whether the image is a JPEG, GIF, or PNG file
- Your search will only return raster images

Using Google image search outside of Prezi

If you have a bit more time available when searching for imagery, then you might decide to open a web browser and run a Google image search outside of Prezi. If so, here are some tips that will definitely help.

Advanced image search

Most "Non-Masters" will simply go to the Google images home page, type in a keyword and click search. Those of us in the know, however, will normally always click on the **Advanced search** option to the right of the screen and fine-tune our search before selecting an image.

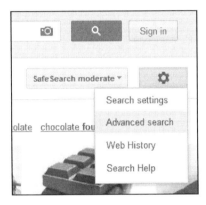

This can actually save your time in the long run because you can be very clear about what you want to see.

Some options I would definitely take advantage of in the advanced image search are:

- **Set Image size** to larger than 800 x 600 pixels. Chances are that these images won't be pixilated as much when zoomed into in Prezi.

- **Type of image** should be set to **Photo** to save you scrolling through hideous clip art images.

> A Prezi master will never use clip art. Unless your Prezi is titled "Look how bad clip art is!" I'd recommend you stay well away from it.

- **Color in image** is extremely useful if you're trying to create a particular style throughout your Prezi and want all imagery to use the same color scheme.

- **Usage rights** should always have the **Only images labeled for reuse** option selected. This works the same as the Prezi pre-license option and lowers the risk of you inserting copyrighted imagery.
- **File Type** can be set to only look for .png, .jpg, or .gif formats which are useful if, for example, you want to take advantage of transparent backgrounds in PNG files.

Standard search

If you decide not to use the advanced search option and simply type your keyword, cross your fingers, and hope for the best, then make sure you look at the following before saving and inserting an image into Prezi.

By simply rolling your mouse over one of the images in your Google search, you can reveal some key information about that image file. The key things you should look for are the **file type** and the **dimensions**.

The reason I've selected the image shown in the preceding screenshot in my search is because I can see it's a PNG file, which means it will have a transparent background once inserted into Prezi. The file also has a dimension of 500 x 400 pixels. Normally I'd look for something bigger, but I know that I won't be zooming into this image in my Prezi, so for now this will do.

Google image search limitations

You will need to save the image somewhere on your PC, and then go back into Prezi to insert it. This obviously takes time.

- You cannot use Google image search to find vector files compatible with Prezi, that is, SWF or PDF files.

Other online sources for imagery

If getting that perfect image in your Prezi is important to you (as it should be), then there are other sources you may want to turn to other than Google images. The web has hundreds of online image libraries just waiting to be tapped into. If you still want your images completely free, then www.sxc.hu and www.morguefile.com are definitely worth checking out. There are also some outstanding premium resources available that give the highest quality images taken by professional photographers. Obviously such resources aren't going to be free, but if you're building your Prezi for business use, I'm hoping you might have some budget for a small spend to get your Prezi looking great.

Here are some things you should know about using online image libraries.

Bang for your buck

A simple online search for "Image Library" will bring up the most popular resources. These will no doubt include the following:

- www.shutterstock.com
- www.gettyimages.co.uk
- www.istockphoto.com

There are obviously many other that you may wish to look into, but if you are going to invest in the right image, then make sure you get the biggest bang for your buck and compare the following before signing up to any of these sites:

- Is there a "Pay Per Download" option? You don't want to be paying a monthly subscription unless you're a designer and need tons of images regularly.
- Do you get access to any free images when signing up?
- How much are the highest resolution images?

 Most sites will use a credits system, so make sure you know how many credits you need for the top quality images, as it's these that you'll want to use in Prezi.

The big advantage

When you read that these online resources needed to be paid for, you might have instantly thought "Oh well, I'll skip this part", and I wouldn't have thought any less of you. However, I'm glad you're still reading this because there are some major benefits that these resources can bring to your Prezi designs:

- **Time saving**: These sites make their money by giving you fast access to the images you want, so the advanced search facilities are usually very detailed and you won't end up scrolling through hundreds of images that aren't related to your original search.

- **Vector images**: All of these libraries will allow you to search for vector images as well as raster. This is obviously a massive advantage, if you're planning to zoom in on images and want to keep everything looking great.

- **Other media**: Although their main focus might be imagery, these resources will no doubt stock video, music, and animations as well. All of which can really bring your Prezi to life, which we'll discuss in later chapters.

Time versus quality

To summarize this section, the following chart shows you the three methods mentioned previously and the effects that using either of them will have on your Prezi design.

Method for finding imagery	How this affects your Prezi
Prezi from web function	Fastest method of finding imagery, but only searches for raster imagery without displaying the file type or size.
Google image search online	Allows for a more advanced search, but it does mean that you have to save the image outside of Prezi and then insert it, which can take time.
Online image library	Will have a price attached, but gives the option of searching for vector and raster images that have been produced by professional photographers and/or designers, giving your Prezi a stunning look and feel.

The best of both worlds

Hopefully, this far into the chapter, you understand the obvious benefits that both raster and vector imagery bring. But what if you could combine the best of both worlds and have a realistic looking imagery like photographs, at a very small file size, with the ability to zoom into them as far as you like with no pixilation at all? Well guess what, you can!

In the rest of this chapter you'll learn how to become a true master and create imagery that has amazing style, as well as being perfect for use in Prezi. You don't need to buy any expensive software to do this, or have a degree in graphic design.

Two separate methods are explained further for turning raster images into vector so that they look great and load quickly in Prezi. The only difference between these methods is that one is completely free, and the other has a small price attached.

Vectorising your imagery

In the steps that follow, you'll learn how to turn a raster image into a stunning looking vector version. You'll be able to do this without spending a penny on expensive software, so it's a great benefit to your Prezis, and your budget!

1. First of all, you'll need a good raster image to vectorise. If you don't already have something to use, then we'd suggest a quick search on Google images for something interesting.

    To continue with the current theme (and to give you another sugar rush), we'll use the raster image of chocolate squares, that you've seen earlier in the chapter. This should look even yummier once it's turned into a vector graphic and inserted into Prezi.

2. Now you need to do download and install Inkscape which is a great piece of vector editing software mentioned earlier in this chapter. It's completely open source which makes it free for anyone to download and use. Inkscape is available on Windows and Macintosh platforms, and has very similar capabilities to its more expensive cousin Adobe Illustrator!

 If you'd like to learn more about Inkscape you can purchase a copy of *Bethany Hiitola's* book, *Inkscape Beginners Guide* from Packt Publishing.

Go to `http://www.inkscape.org/`and click on the **Download** section to install the correct version of Inkscape for your operating system.

Once the software is installed, you should see the Inkscape icon in your programs list or on your desktop.

3. Now for the fun bit! Obviously, we won't go into detail on all of Inkscape's many features, but it's time to open the software and vectorise your image.

    Double-click the Inkscape icon from your list of programs.

4. When the software opens, go to the **File** menu and click on **IMPORT**.

5. Select your raster image and click on **OK**.

6. Make sure the **embed** option is selected on the next screen and click on **OK**.

    When your image appears on the Inkscape page, make sure it is selected and surrounded by arrows as shown in the following screenshot:

7. Now go to **Path** and select **TRACEBITMAP**. The pop-up box that appears will allow you to create a vector trace of your raster image.

    ○   If your image is a simple line drawing without much color, then adjust the settings in the top half of the screen under **Single scan**. Click on **UPDATE** to see a preview, and then on **OK** to create the vector trace.

○ If your image is a color photo like the one in the previous step, you'll need to concentrate on the lower half of the **Trace Bitmap** screen. Select **Colors**, click on **UPDATE**, and adjust settings further until you are happy with the preview. Click on **OK** to create your trace.

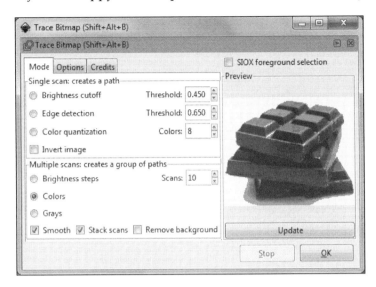

8. Back on the main screen, you will see the new vector version of your image. Hold the *Ctrl* key and use your mouse wheel to zoom in, or click the **up arrow** in the **z** box bottom-right corner of the screen.

9. If you aren't happy with the vector, just delete it and repeat the steps. Adjust the settings in the **Trace Bitmap** screen until you are happy.

Once you are happy with the trace, click on the new vector and move it to one side. You'll see the original raster below. Delete the raster image leaving only the vector onscreen.

10. Now go to **File** and select **Save As**. Select **Portable Document Format (*.pdf)** from the **Save as type** drop-down list, and save your new vector image to your desktop.

Commit to being a master

On opening Inkscape for the first time, you might be overwhelmed by all of the various buttons and options available. Don't be put off by these, and if you can, we'd really recommend you take some time to explore Inkscape in more detail. There are many other useful tools within the software that will really make you into a master of creating imagery for Prezi. Don't get scared – get curious.

11. Now it's time to insert your new vector image into Prezi. Our guess is you probably got so excited at the end of step 3 that you've already done it, but just in case you need the instructions to complete this process, keep reading further.

    ○ Open Prezi and click on **Insert** from the bubble menu.

    ○ Click on **Image** and then click on **Select files** to find your vector image.

    ○ Select your vector image and click **OPEN**.

    ○ Once the image is on your Prezi canvas, you can use the zoom tools to go in as close as you like without any loss of image.

The quick way

If you really don't have the time to go through the preceding steps every time you need to create a vector image, then follow the next set of steps. It's much quicker, but unfortunately it does come at a cost.

Hopefully you enjoyed the last exercise, and learned lots during the process. You might be sitting at your desk now thinking "That's amazing, but will I have time to do this for 20 images?" We appreciate that you are probably working to very tight deadlines forced upon you by your business, and although there might be a small cost involved, the time saving will pay off in the long run.

Just like in the previous steps, you'll need another raster image to vectorise. You can either use the same image as you did before, or carry out another Google Image search for something interesting.

1. Go to http://www.vectormagic.com and click the **Upload Image To Trace** button.

2. Select the raster image you'd like to vectorise and click **OK**.

3. Vector Magic will then perform a trace for you and compare the raster and vector image onscreen.

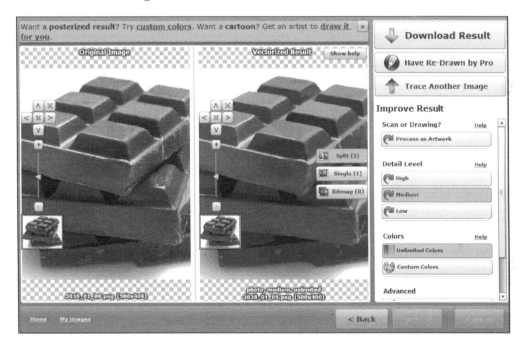

4. The default settings of Vector Magic are normally very good, so if you are happy with them click **Download result**.

5. You'll be asked to enter an e-mail address so that you can set up a free account.

6. Once you have verified the account, select the **PDF** option for download, and save it to your desktop.

7. Open Prezi and click on **Insert** from the bubble menu.

8. Click on **Image** and then click on **Select files** to find your vector image.

9. Select your vector image and click on **OPEN**.

10. Once the image is on your Prezi canvas, you can use the zoom tools to zoom in as close as you like, without any loss of image.

As you can see from the previous two methods, there are some clear benefits for each, but an obvious difference in the amount of time and effort it will take. Only you will be able to decide which method suits you and the demands of your business.

One thing is for sure though. Vector imagery lends itself much better to building presentations in Prezi and you should try to use it wherever you can.

Creating your own flavor

If you have even the tiniest of creative bones in your body, then you might be able to take your Prezi designs to an even higher level by creating your very own illustrations, and vectorising them for Prezi.

Just like you, we've also been shackled by the time restraints of business at some point in our careers. Let's pretend the boss of your company BIG Mechanics is giving an important presentation in an hour's time, and he's kindly tasked you with pulling together something really eye-catching that explains how the company is like a giant machine with lots of dials and cogs that all work together in unison to get results. You know the same old business talk we've heard a million times before!

So once he's finished telling you what he needs, you now only have 40 minutes left. What would be perfect is an image of a giant machine with the company name on it, but can you find a decent enough raster image in time? You'll then need to vectorise it, add the company name to it somehow and then insert it into Prezi. That's going to be a challenge, so why not use your imagination, and create the exact image you need from scratch?

Grab a pen

While we can't teach you how to be a world class illustrator in this chapter, we do hope to give you enough confidence to at least have a go at this. When vectorised and inserted into Prezi illustrations look great, and the fact that they are your own work gives your Prezi a much more human touch. Here's how to vectorise your own illustrations:

1. Grab a decent pen that isn't going to run out of ink and has a fairly thick nib. Try and use your company's corporate color if you can.

2. Draw your image on plain white paper.

3. Get the image onto your PC using a scanner or digital camera.

4. Use Inkscape or Vector Magic to trace the image and create a vector version.

5. Save as a PDF file.

6. Insert into Prezi.

Obviously, we are all going to be of different skill levels when it comes to drawing our own illustrations, but even a badly drawn image seems to look a little nicer once vectorised and inserted into Prezi.

 Make sure you have a try at vectorising your own illustrations. If you get even slightly good at it, then you'll save time, and also have one of a kind imagery for your Prezis.

Working with images – quick tips

If your Prezi is using lots of images, here are a couple of tips worth knowing:

1. If there are areas of the image you don't want your audience to see, then simply double-click the image and drag the corners that appear to crop the unwanted area out as shown in the following screenshot:

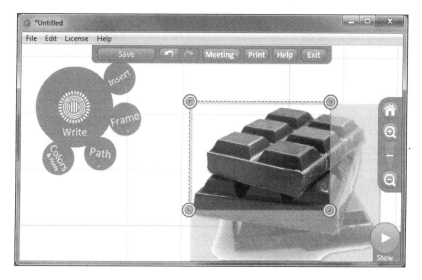

To place images on top of one another in the correct order, you can simply right-click on your PC, or press *Ctrl+click* for Mac, on an image and select one of the four available options to change its position.

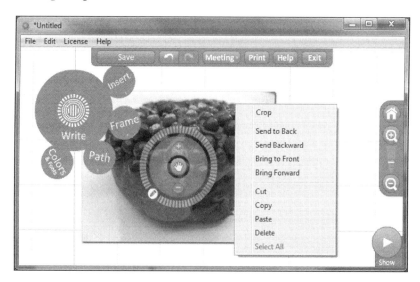

Summary

Hopefully, you've found this chapter extremely useful, and are well on your way to mastering the techniques described previously.

We've looked at the differences between raster and vector imagery, where to find the best images, and also how to create your own that work in the best way possible for a Prezi presentation.

Remember though that business presentations need to deliver important messages on time, and as effectively as possible. With this in mind, it's crucial that you decide just how much time you're going to spend on imagery when you also need to consider other important factors, and probably juggle other projects.

Give yourself enough time and do Prezi the justice it deserves to really make an impact in your business presentations. Don't rely on the fact that people will be wowed by the zooming and spinning if they haven't seen Prezi before. This won't last long and certainly won't deliver your message any more clearly.

Make sure you project the right image.

Now that you've mastered imagery in Prezi, it's time to look at using sound as well. The skills you've learned in this chapter will help the visual learners in your audience understand your presentation, but what about the auditory learners in the crowd who need a little extra help?

In *Chapter 2, Using Audio*, we'll address the use of audio in Prezi and also highlight some of the software's current limitations in this area. Whether you're standing in front of an audience and presenting or embedding your Prezi into a website for people to explore online and in their own time, sound can really help.

2
Using Audio

There's more to delivering a presentation than just making it look great with some snazzy imagery. Sure we can stimulate the audience visually to help them understand our message, but a lot of thought also needs to be given as to what they hear. A lot of your audience may have a very auditory learning style, and so it's important we try and factor this into our Prezi designs as well.

In this chapter, you'll learn how to add sound to your Prezi files, and become aware of some important points to think about when in the design stage. Topics to be covered include:

- How Prezi plays sound
- Using the `.swf` or `.wmv` files for sound
- Adding background music
- Using sound at specific points in your Prezi

Why use sound in Prezi?

Apart from the reasons mentioned previously, your Prezi will really benefit from having sound if you decide to embed it into a website or share it on the Prezi explore page (`http://prezi.com/explore/`). There's more detail on this in *Chapter 6, Prezis for Online Delivery*, but making Prezi files that people can explore on their own is a huge benefit to people that might not have had the time to be at your live presentation. Adding sound into these online Prezis will help the users exploring them understand the content quicker and with more clarity.

You might decide to have audio recorded from your live session and have it played at certain points in your Prezi. Or you might just want to create some kind of mood for the user that fits with your Prezis message. For the latter, you can use a music track that loops continuously when your Prezi is viewed online.

A great example of sound being used to its full potential in Prezi can be seen on the Prezi Explore page at `http://prezi.com/wwmfvms6dno-/the-maverick-presenter-prezihelpcom/`.

Some other benefits that using sounds can bring are:

- Provides a bigger impact with auditory learners in your session
- Allows expert speakers to talk to your audience without even being there
- Gives people viewing the Prezi online a chance to feel like they were really there at your live event
- Online Prezis could offer translations into multiple languages to be selected and listened to at the user's discretion
- Generally makes a presentation more interesting, engaging, and memorable

Where's the Insert Audio button?

Like any piece of software, there are lots of clever little things happening beneath the surface that we don't see. When you use the Image option on the web and the Google images appear, that's because some lovely person at Prezi wrote some clever coding to make it all happen.

It's these clever little bits of code that mean you can insert shapes, images, frames, movies, drawings, and so on. But where's the insert audio button? Surely the developers at Prezi have thought of that haven't they?

Well actually, no, they haven't. Not yet anyway. At this moment, Prezi is still in its infancy and changing all the time. One thing the Prezi team is great at is listening to their users and introducing new features based on what users want. At this moment in time, there is no insert audio button in Prezi, but it doesn't mean that will be the case forever, and if you really want audio there are ways to add it. Otherwise what would be the point in this chapter!

How is audio inserted?

As you hopefully know by now, Prezi can handle video files (refer the *Chapter 3, Inserting a Video*) and it's this video feature that your audio can piggyback a ride on to end up inside your Prezi file.

The following screenshot should give you a basic understanding of how this is done:

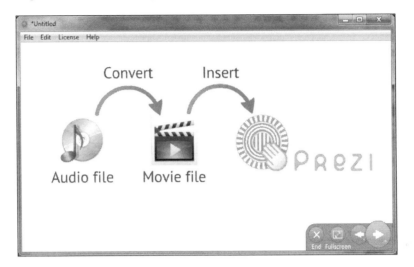

Until inserting audio becomes part of the Prezi software, (fingers crossed it'll be soon) you will have to convert your audio files into video format to use them on your Prezi canvas.

What this means is that the techniques explained in the rest of this chapter are really just a workaround to trick Prezi into thinking you're using video, which technically you will be. It'll all become clear throughout the chapter, and trust us; it will definitely set your Prezis apart from the rest of the crowd and get you to Prezi Master Status.

There are two different routes you can take to use audio in Prezi, so we'll explore them both in detail here and hopefully your Prezis will be making lots of noise by the end of the chapter.

Where to get sound files from?

Knowing where to find great sounds from will save you lots of time, and just like with imagery there are some great online libraries to choose from:

- www.clipdealer.com
- www.sound-effects-library.com
- www.audionetwork.com

Each of these online libraries offers thousands of sound effects and music tracks at very low prices. They all have very easy-to-use search facilities, and for those of you who are aspiring to become a Prezi DJ you can use Audio Networks beats per minute calculator in your search to help you find really fast-paced tracks, or relaxing slow tracks.

Of course you can also search for sound effects and music tracks that are free to download. In some instances, this will take a little longer, but ultimately means that you and your company aren't spending a penny and achieving some great results.

Here's the best of the free audio libraries:

* `http://www.freesound.org`
* `http://www.partnersinrhyme.com`
* `http://www.audiomicro.com`

Creating your own sounds

You probably won't have time to sit there in the office and create your own sound effects of babies crying, dogs barking, and a T-Rex roaring. If you do, then please don't blame us when your boss calls you into his office because they think you're having a breakdown!

If you want to add narration to your Prezi, or maybe have a subject matter expert speak to your audience without flying them in from halfway around the world, then you can use the following technique to record and edit your own sound files for free.

1. Go to `http://audacity.sourceforge.net` and download the free audio recording software.

2. Install the software onto your PC or laptop and then install the LAME encoder from `http://manual.audacityteam.org/help/manual/man/faq_installation_and_plug_ins.html#lame`. This enables you to export your sounds in the `.mp3` format.

3. Now open **Audacity**. When you first open the software it will detect your machines microphone.

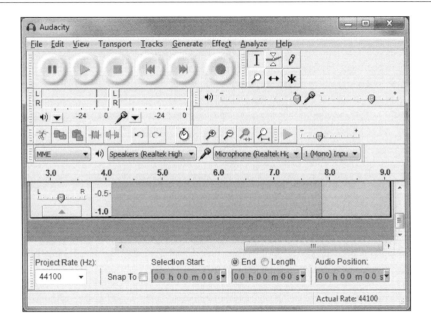

 Try not to be phased by the amount of buttons and functions in the software. For now, we'll just focus on the record button, and export function.

4. Click on the **Record** button to start recording your audio, and click on the **Stop** button when you're finished.

5. Click on the **Play** button to review the sound and the **Delete** button on your keyboard to remove it and start again.

6. Once you're happy with your audio, click on **File, Export**, and select **WAV** from the file type drop-down list.

7. Open your exported **WAV** file to test it. Repeat steps 4-6 to create additional audio files.

If you do want colleagues from overseas or subject matter experts to speak in your Prezi, then you'll need to send the preceding instructions to them unless they already have the capabilities to record their voice.

Unfortunately, creating the sound is only the first step, and as you'll see further, there is more that's needed to get audio working well inside Prezi.

 Learning more about Audacity

To learn more about Audacity and its many functions, go to http://audacity.sourceforge.net/manual-1.2/tutorials.html.

Audio options

There are two ways of using sound in your Prezi. You can have looping background music, or you can have sounds that just play once at certain path points in your Prezi. There are obvious benefits to using both of these different options whether your Prezi is being showed online or in front of a live audience. By teaching you these techniques, it's our hope that you'll be able to come up with some really creative uses for sound that really take your Prezi skills to the next level.

Option 1 – looping the background music

Now obviously if you're delivering to a live audience and want background music you can just use your laptop or another audio device separated from your Prezi. That will save you the time and effort of trying to build it into your Prezi file, and of course in business, time is money. But what happens after the live presentation when people ask you "Can we have the presentation to review?"

Wouldn't it be great to give them exactly the same experience they had in the live session and to use the same music, or at least some background music to help set the mood for your presentation?

Your average Joe Prezi user would probably pass on this to save time. But a Prezi Master would make their Prezi as memorable as possible, even if it's being viewed without them.

When to add background sound?

We'd recommend you complete this step at the end of your Prezi design. Once the sound is inserted in this way it is difficult to remove, so make sure everything in your Prezi is perfect before you add any background music. It's also a good idea to save a backup version of your Prezi, just in case.

What you need for Option 1?

If you are extremely lucky and have a copy of Adobe Flash in your organization, then you can use that to insert your music into and create a Shockwave Flash file (.swf) file that will then be inserted into Prezi.

When inserted into Prezi the .swf file will automatically start to play, and will loop continuously throughout. It won't matter where in the Prezi your users are, the music will still be playing.

For the purpose of this exercise, we'll assume that not everyone is so lucky to have Adobe Flash, and that you'd rather know how to add background music for free.

There are a few things you'll need to complete the task of adding background sound:

- Windows Live Movie Maker (Free)
- AVS Video Converter (Free at `http://www.avs4you.com/index.aspx`)
- An audio file (Your music)
- A small image so you can identify the music once inserted into Prezi

Creating a movie

The following steps will help you create a movie file that plays music throughout. You'll learn how to add an image to the file so that it's easy to spot and move around once you finally get it into Prezi.

1. Open **Windows Live Movie Maker**.

2. Click on **Add videos and photos** and select the image you've chosen to identify your sound in Prezi. A speaker icon is usually an obvious choice.

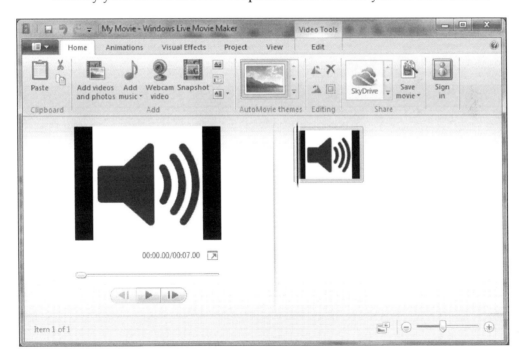

3. Click on the **Add music** button to add your audio file as well. You will then see the name of your music file above the image icon in Windows Live Movie Maker.

4. Go to the **Project** tab and click on **Fit to Music**. This means your image will be seen through the entire length of your audio file.

5. Click on the **Save movie** button and select the **Recommended for this project** option. This will save your movie as a Windows Media Video (.wmv) file.

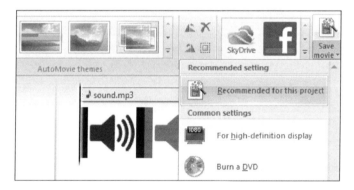

Converting to .swf

The following instructions will help you convert your Windows movie file into a .swf so that it continuously loops when inserted into Prezi.

1. Open AVS Video Converter.

2. Click on the **To SWF** button in the **Formats** tab on top of the screen.

3. Click on the **Browse...**button on the right of the **InputFileName** textbox and select the movie you created in Windows Live Movie Maker.

4. Click on the **Browse...**button on the right of the **OutputFileName** textbox and select the destination for your converted file to end up in.

5. Click on **Convert now** to start the conversion to a .swf file.

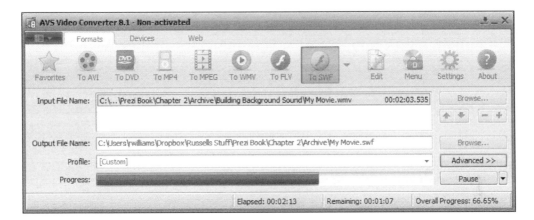

 Once the file is converted to the .swf format open it up in a web browser to check if it works fine.

The Prezi bit

Finally, you're ready to insert the .swf file into your Prezi canvas. Make sure you follow the following steps to finish the process.

1. Save a backup of your finished Prezi before you insert the .swf file.

 This is good practice regardless of whether you're inserting sound or not.

2. In Prezi, click on **Insert** and then click on **File**.

3. Select your new .swf file.

4. Move the file somewhere on the canvas so that it won't be seen by your audience, but keep a note of where you've placed it.

5. Save your Prezi file.

 To know the difference between your finished Prezis with and without audio, it's a good idea to add something into the naming scheme you use. An example might be MyPrezi_v0.1 and MyPrezi_v0.1_Audio.

Testing the audio

To test that your audio file is going to work properly, put your Prezi into show mode by clicking on the **Show** button in the bottom right of your canvas.

As soon as the .swf file loads, the music will start to play. You can continue through your Prezis paths or explore the canvas freely, and you'll still hear the continuous loop of your music.

Sharing your Prezi

Sharing your Prezis online is explored more in *Chapter 6, Prezis for Online Delivery*, but here is the quickest way to ensure that everyone in your organization can view your Prezi.

To share your Prezi using the Prezi desktop editor, do the following:

1. Inside Prezi desktop, go to **File** and select **UploadtoPrezi.com**.
2. Enter the title of your Prezi and a short description, and then click on **Upload**.

3. When the upload is complete, click on the link displayed to access your Prezi online.

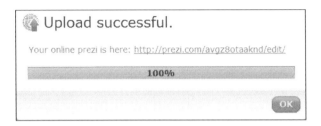

4. Now click on the **Share** button located just below the Prezi to open the share dialogue box.

5. Click on the **Copy** button to copy the URL for viewing this Prezi online, and e-mail it to your colleagues.

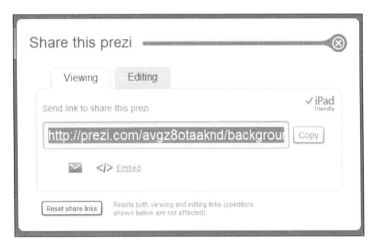

Although the steps that you have just gone through may seem a little long winded, there's no doubt that knowing how to add background sound into Prezi will take you from novice to master, especially when there isn't an easy "Insert sound" option available in the software itself.

As with all the techniques described in this book, you will have to decide whether or not the business payoff is great enough to warrant the time it may take to complete certain tasks.

Option 2 – different sounds at path points

This is without a doubt one of the best ways to add some real flare to your Prezi.

By adding sound at certain path points in your Prezi, you can add narration to your story, allow subject matter experts to talk to your audience, or use background noise to help explain certain environments you're discussing, that is, busy warehouses, supermarkets, call centers, and sales floors.

The possibilities are all down to your own creativity, but let's get started and get your Prezi doing the talking for you.

What you need for Option 2?

Just as you did earlier, you'll need to open Windows Live Movie Maker and create a movie file. This time we won't need to convert it to `.swf` as the standard `.wmv` format will suffice.

To get the sounds to play inside Prezi, you will need to link your path points directly to them. Because of this, make sure the image you use in Windows Live Movie Maker makes it very obvious what your sound file is. That will make it easier for you to move things around in your Prezi.

For the purpose of this exercise we've used the sound and image of a cat, and the sound and image of a dog. If you're using subject matter experts who say more than woof woof or meow, then you might decide to use a photo of them so that your audience can connect better with the voice. If you can't find a good enough image to use there is an extra step at the end that explains how to hide the sound files behind other content in your Prezi while it plays.

So all you need is:

- Windows Live Movie Maker
- Audio files
- An image to help you identify the audio once inserted into Prezi

Creating a movie

Make sure you follow the given steps in order to create your movie file that contains the sounds you need. These first few steps are the same as the previous exercise, but the steps that follow mean we can change the way that Prezi interacts with the sound files.

1. Open Windows Live Movie Maker.
2. Click on **Add videos and photos** and select the image you've chosen to identify your sound in Prezi.

3. Click on the **Add music** button to add your audio file as well. You will then see the name of your audio file above the image icon in Windows Live Movie Maker.

4. Go to the **Project** tab and click on **Fit to Music**. This means your image will be seen through the entire length of your audio file

5. Click on the **Save movie** button and select the **Recommended for this project** option. This will save your movie as a Windows Media Video (.wmv) file.

Inserting into Prezi

Now that we have the sounds we need in the form of a movie file, it's very easy to get them onto our Prezi canvas. The following steps explain how to make each sound play at certain points during your presentation.

1. In Prezi, go to **Insert** and select **File**.

2. Select your .wmv file and click on **Open**.

3. Once the .wmv file is loaded, use the **Path** button to link it to the path of your Prezi.

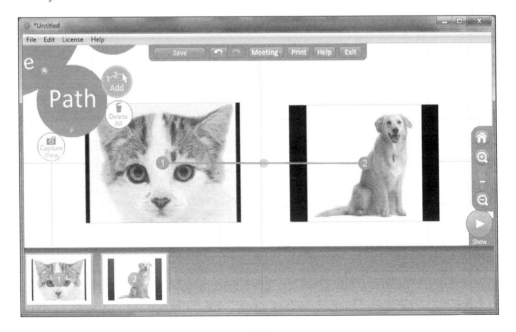

4. Click on the **Show** button or press the *spacebar* and then click on the *right arrow* on your keyboard to travel along your path. The sound should play automatically when you reach it.

Hiding sound behind content (optional)

Only use this step if you want to display other content while your sound plays. It might be that you want to use a better image, or display bullet pointed text.

1. Create a blank image that is of the same color as your Prezi canvas background and save it as a .png or .jpg file.

2. In Prezi, click on **Insert** and select **Image** to insert the blank image on top of the audio file.

3. Double-click on the blank image to resize it and make sure it completely covers your audio file.

4. Now enter any text or imagery you want to display on top of the blank image.

 You do not need to adjust any of the path points we created earlier.

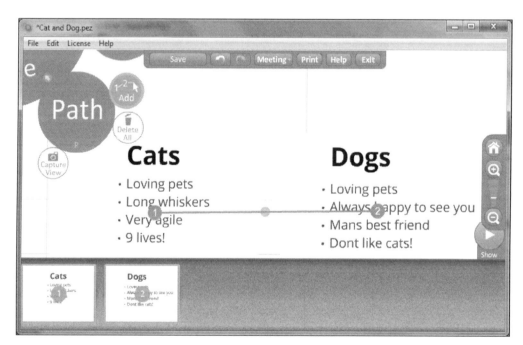

Now the sound files are hidden behind text.

The paths you have already created will stay as they are in order to activate the audio file and make sure it plays, but by adding these layers of content on top of the audio file you can give your audience a lot more to see and hear which makes for a much more engaging experience for both visual and auditory learning styles.

Being clever with audio

Hopefully by this stage you have a great understanding of how to get sound into your Prezi, and of course what the limitations on the software might be. But how is this going to make your presentations better and more memorable? A few ways that sound can be used in your Prezi are discussed in this chapter.

Translation

If you are part of a large global organization or if you have an international customer base then you might decide to build a Prezi that can be embedded into your company website for colleagues and customers to explore on their own.

The obvious way to use sound here would be to have some nice background music that plays throughout, and have any text displayed in several different languages. The problem with that is that you'll end up with lots and lots of text in your Prezi which doesn't make for nice viewing.

A Prezi Master would use hardly any text at all and let their Prezi do the talking for them by inserting separate audio translations that the user could click on on their own.

The aesthetics of how you chose to display the different translations are up to you but obviously we'd suggest using flags or the symbol of each country that's available to the online user and repeating the steps mentioned earlier to create separate .wmv files for each piece of audio.

Narration

We've already mentioned having subject matter experts talk to your audience, but if your Prezi is part of a training program or may be a staff induction then using narration at various points could be extremely powerful.

You might design a Prezi and deliver a presentation to colleagues yourself, but you could reinforce the message by using the same Prezi file and adding narration, then sending out the link for everyone to view it.

Or you might have a business critical process that needs explaining quickly to colleagues around the world. Create a Prezi with narration, share it online and save yourself the airfares!

Using this technique you could start to build an entire library of business processes, inductions, and training that your colleagues are able to explore in their own time.

Creating an environment

When new members of staff join your business they normally spend a few days in a classroom environment having training. There's a projector and a whiteboard, and for the most part they engage in good conversations with the trainer and each other and learn a lot.

But then when they hit the retail shop floor or the sales floor of your busy call center they feel slightly overwhelmed. This is mainly due to the fact that their training environment is very different from the real thing.

So why not use sound in your training induction Prezis to create the same kind of atmosphere? It doesn't have to be constant noise throughout the induction but by giving them a flavor of how their working environment will sound, you can help prepare them for the real thing.

If your training induction has lots of activities that involve the new staff thinking and working as a team under pressure then giving them the same sounds that they'll hear every day will really help.

Customers

Along with introducing everyday background noise, why not give your audience sound clips of the types of customers they'll have to deal with.

This is a great way to make role plays much more engaging, and if you design the Prezi well enough you could even give alternative outcomes from the customer interaction depending on the type of response that the training delegate gives.

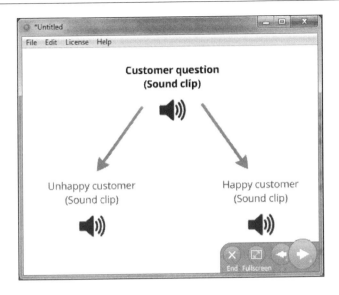

Summary

It's at this point we hope you're now itching to take what you've learned and find excuses to build it into your next Prezi.

As we mentioned at the very start of the chapter, inserting sound into Prezi is not yet a feature of the software. Because of this the vast majority of users don't include sound into their Prezis.

By using the techniques in this chapter, you can help achieve two things:

1. Make yourself look like a true Master of Prezi.
2. Make other Prezi users want to do the same.

The knock on effect of the second point is that when many users together want to insert sound the chances are that Prezi will do their very best to make sure it gets built into the software.

For now though you can enjoy basking in the glory of your incredible sounding Prezis.

In the following chapter, it's time to take a look at how video can really make your Prezis shine and make them even more memorable.

If a picture says a thousand words, then moving pictures with sounds must speak in volumes.

Inserting a Video

3

So far, we've looked at using imagery and sound to grab your audience's attention. It stands to reason that video is going to be even more engaging because it's a combination of these two elements.

Used correctly in Prezi, video can give your audience the most engaging experience, and it can really help get your messages across in a memorable way.

There are lots of different approaches you can take to find or even build your own videos for Prezi and this chapter we will help you understand those approaches, along with how they might fit into your business.

We'll cover the following:

- Technicalities of using video in Prezi
- Searching for and using YouTube videos
- Creating your own YouTube account
- Editing your own videos

The technical bit

As you may already understand from the previous chapter, Prezi has its own built-in video player. Of course, the player sits behind the scenes of your Prezi canvas, so we never actually see it. What we do see are the videos playing beautifully in whichever format we've chosen to use. These might include the following movie file types:

- WMV*
- MOV*
- AVI*
- F4V

- FLV*
- MPG*
- MP4
- M4V
- 3GP
- YouTube videos*

 We could bore you with the explanations of how each file type is different, but we're pretty sure you'd soon switch off. For now, just know that the ones you'll probably come across the most are marked with an *

File size restrictions

If you are the proud owner of a **Pro** or **Edu Pro** license, then you'll be pleased to know there are no file size restrictions at all placed upon your video files.

 Remember the bigger the Prezi file size, the harder it will be to carry on a memory stick and/or share with your colleagues. Try to keep file size down wherever you can.

However, if you use a **Public, Enjoy,** or **Edu Enjoy** license you will be restricted to inserting videos no larger than 50 megabytes. This is simply because those license types rely on using the online Prezi editor to build your Prezis and that means file size has to be kept in check.

Online or offline?

There are a few things you need to know about your Prezi design before you decide on which video format is going to be best for you. These questions are very simple, but if they aren't given any thought at the very start, you could end up in all sorts of trouble!

Will your Prezi be viewed online?

If your Prezi can be viewed online, then you can really take advantage of the insert YouTube option within the software. This means you'll be able to easily insert video without having to worry about huge file size or have to wait forever for it to upload onto your canvas.

To take advantage of using YouTube for video, you'll need to spend some time searching for the right clip or create your own YouTube account and upload your video to it. Both of these techniques are covered in more detail further on in the chapter.

Will colleagues want a copy of your Prezi?

If you know that colleagues will want a copy of your Prezi and that they may even want to make changes to it, then you will need to keep a very close eye on the file size of your videos.

If your organization is using the **Prezi Pro** license and desktop application, then you'll have no restrictions on the video file size you can insert. But no one wants to sit for ten minutes while your 4 gigabyte Prezi file copies to their desktop from the company's server, and you certainly won't be able to e-mail a file of that size.

Ask the question

Following is a quick summary of questions you might want to consider before you begin your Prezi design. The X indicates the preferred option.

Questions	Your own "offline" video files	YouTube videos
You are the only person who will present your Prezi from the desktop player.	X	
You are presenting the Prezi, but others will need to view it online afterwards.		X
The Prezi is only for people to view online and in their own time.		X
The video used is sensitive and not for view by the general public.	X	

Playing videos

Before we look at the different ways of using a video, let's just cover the basics. Once a video is inserted into Prezi, you can decide how and when it plays.

Playing along a path

If you want the video to play automatically, then you'll need to add it to a path just like we did with the audio files from *Chapter 2, Using Audio*.

By simply selecting the video file on your Prezi canvas and clicking paths from the Zebra Menu, you can add the video to your sequence of paths. This will mean the video plays automatically once this point is reached in your presentation.

 Linking the path to a frame that surrounds your video will not make the video play. The path point must be attached to the actual video file or YouTube clip.

Letting the user play

You might decide early on that your Prezi isn't going to use a path, and instead the user can explore on their own and play the videos as and when they chose. If this is the case, then all you need to do is insert the video onto your canvas and make sure the user will see it and know what to do with it.

You could use a simple arrow, as shown in the following screenshot, to point out where the play button is.

We'd also suggest giving the videos a heading by simply dragging a rectangle of color along the top of the video file and typing over the top, as shown in the following screenshot:

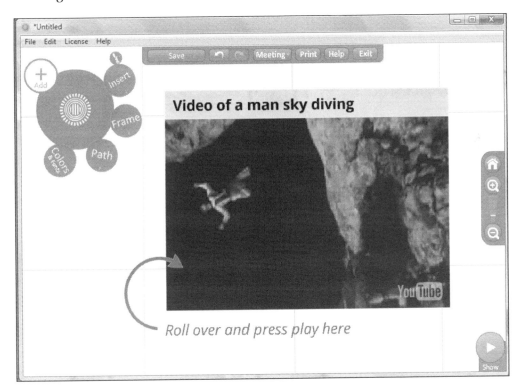

Positioning videos

As with any other elements you might insert into Prezi, the same rules apply when positioning your video file.

By simply selecting the video file, you can scale it up or down in size, spin it around at any angle, and even bring it forward to be above other elements or below them.

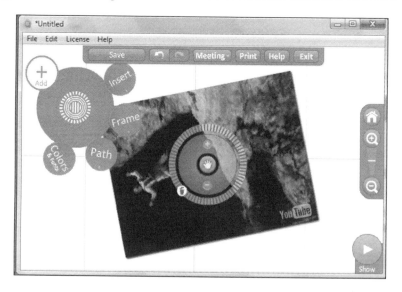

Now that the basics are covered in the rest of this chapter we'll explore different methods for creating, editing, and inserting videos into Prezi.

Videos – the easy way with YouTube

There's no doubt that the easiest and quickest way to use video in your Prezi is by using the Insert YouTube option from the main menu. YouTube has millions of videos available and it would probably take you about 400 years to watch every single video that's stored there.

With such an expansive free source of videos available, it's bound to be your first stop. We'll start from here and add more detail as we go through the chapter.

Be a master

Make sure you explore everything in this chapter and go beyond simply inserting YouTube clips that already exist into your Prezi canvas. You picked up this book because you wanted to master Prezi and all of the elements it can contain so stick with it and give everything mentioned a try.

Searching for the right clip

So you've come to a point in your Prezi where a video would be a really useful source of stimulation for your audience. But how do you find the right clip and insert it into your Prezi canvas?

Let's pretend we need a short clip of someone doing a parachute jump. The clip needs to be a couple of minutes long, and very high quality:

1. Go to www.youtube.com.

2. Enter a keyword or phrase into the **search panel**, for example, **Parachute jump**.

3. Use the **Filter** option to find clips shorter than four minutes and in HD quality.

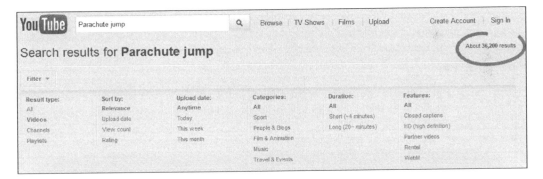

4. Using the filters will decrease the amount of videos available. This is circled in the upper-right corner of the preceding screenshot.

5. Click on a video that looks like a good match and watch it from start to finish, checking the quality.

6. Once you find the clip, copy the URL from the top of the web page.

7. Now go into your Prezi canvas and click on **Insert** and **YouTube** then paste the URL into the dialogue box provided and click on **Insert**.

 To save a little time, you can skip step 6 and paste the URL of your YouTube clip into Prezi as text directly onto your canvas. Prezi will do the rest for you.

It's definitely a good idea to use the filtering system on the YouTube website. By just selecting a couple of filters, you can reduce the amount of videos in your search by a few thousand or even more. This will save you a lot of time and help to give you exactly what you need.

 Using this method does not embed the YouTube clips into your Prezi but simply creates a link to them. In order to use this method, you must be 100 percent certain that when you finally present your Prezi there will be a reliable Internet connection available, and that the YouTube website is not blocked by your IT department.

Creating your own YouTube account

If you have your own videos that you'd like to use, and you know that there will be a reliable Internet connection when it comes to presenting and/or your Prezi will be viewed by people online, then you can really take advantage of the Insert YouTube option and use your own videos.

Uploading your own videos to YouTube

It will definitely be beneficial for you to create your very own YouTube account. If you already have a Google account, then you'll be able to use those details to access YouTube. If not, then just click the **Create Account** button from the home page and enter your e-mail address and details. There are lots of benefits to having your own YouTube account, but the main one for you right now is the fact that you'll be able to upload your own video files and then link them to your Prezi canvas. This saves you the time required for inserting large video files directly into your Prezi and increasing the file size.

There are a number of ways to create your own video files, from using a smart phone that films in high definition to a digital camera or professional video camera. However way you create your videos, you'll soon see that you can improve their quality a lot when you upload them to YouTube.

Once your account is created, follow these steps to upload your own videos:

1. Click on the **Upload** link located at the top of the screen.
2. Select the video file from your computer.
3. Give the video a title. The **Description** and **Category** fields are optional.
4. Make sure you select the **Unlisted** option under the **Privacy** settings. This will mean your Prezi can play the clip, but the video isn't viewable by the general public on YouTube.

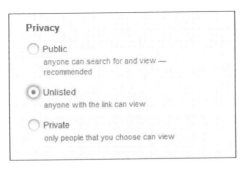

5. Once the video is uploaded, copy the link and insert the YouTube clip into your Prezi.

Editing videos in YouTube

A great feature of YouTube is that you can edit videos once they've been uploaded and give those titles, captions, speech bubbles, and even special effects. This will really help give you that professional looking edge and help give all of your videos a similar look and feel for use in your Prezi.

1. Click on the **Video Manager** link located under your username in the upper-right corner of the site.
2. Then click on the **Edit** button under the video you'd like to make changes to.

3. You'll then be taken to the **Info and Settings** page of your video and from here you can access the editing features.

Enhancements

Accessing the enhancements area will automatically play you two versions of your video. One is the original, while the other is a quick preview of what any changes you select will look like. In this area you can improve colors and the brightness of your video. You can also trim the start and end of the video that might have unnecessary delays in order to make things very slick.

There are three sub headings within the enhancements area:

- Quick Fixes
- Effects
- Audio

Quick Fixes

The **Quick Fixes** menu allows you to very easily adjust the color settings of your video by adjusting the scales for **Lightness, Contrast, Saturation,** and **Color Temperature** as shown in the following screenshot:

When you adjust any of these options, you will automatically get to see a preview of the changes to decide if they are of benefit or not. The **I'm Feeling Lucky** button will adjust all of the above settings for you, based on what it thinks needs improving.

Also in the enhancements area, you can use the **Trim** button to remove pauses at the start or end of your video. Rotate your video to the left or right depending on the camera angle it was shot at. And you can also use the **Stabilise** button to remove any jerky video and smooth things out.

Effects

In this sub menu, you can chose from a handful of effects that have been created for you. This could be useful if you wanted all your videos to match the same look and feel of other imagery in your Prezi.

In the following screenshot, you can see that the **Cartoon** effect has been applied, and the video on the right of the screen is showing a preview of how this will look.

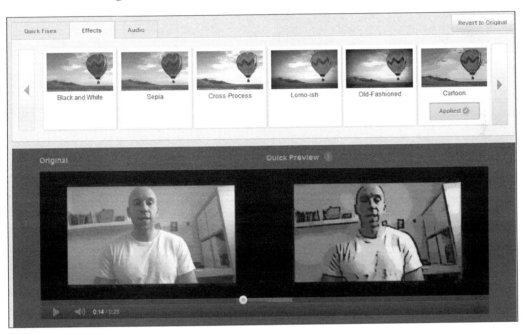

Audio

In this sub menu, you can chose to override the sound in your video with a music track from the YouTube library. There are hundreds to choose from and this can really help for those videos taken outdoors where wind might be the only thing you can hear. This is also another, really nice way of tying the style of your videos and your Prezi together.

There is a very useful option to allow a blend between the music you select and the sound that already exists in your video. The scale shown in the following screenshot can be dragged either way to allow the blending to occur.

Annotations

By moving on to the **Annotations** menu, you now have the option to add **Speech Bubbles**, **Notes**, **Titles**, **Spotlights**, and **Pauses** into your video.

To add any of these annotations click on the **Add annotations** drop-down list on the right of the screen and select which type of annotation you require. In the following screenshot, you can see a **Speech bubble** has been selected.

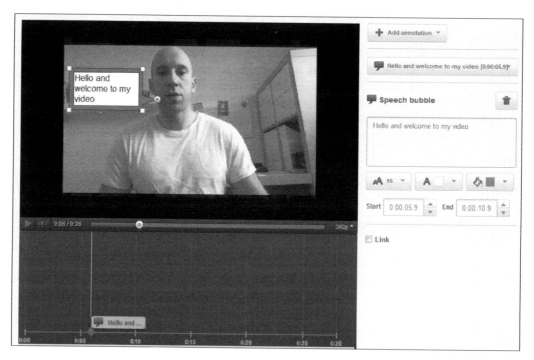

You will then see the **Speech bubble** settings and a textbox to enter the text you want to appear inside the bubble. You can select the color of the bubble and text and drag the corners of the bubble onscreen to adjust its size and shape.

Make sure you get the timings right in the **Start** and **End** options, so that your **Speech bubble** appears and disappears at the right time.

 Use the **Title** annotation at the start of your video to create a nice introduction, and again at the end for credits or instructions to the users on what to do next in your Prezi.

Captions

If you are part of a global organization and you'd like your colleagues overseas to understand your videos, then captions will allow you to add subtitles. This is obviously very useful for those that are hard of hearing as well.

1. Click on the **Captions** menu at the top of the screen.
2. Then click on the word **English** just below **Machine Transcriptions**.

3. In the edit menu that appears, you'll see that YouTube has cleverly converted (although maybe not accurately) your speech into a transcript.
4. Now click on the **Download** button to open the transcript as a text file.
5. When the text file opens, edit the text to read correctly and then save it to your desktop.
6. Make sure you don't delete any of the timestamps within the text.
7. Now back in YouTube, click **Return to All Tracks** and then click **Add New Captions or Transcripts**.
8. Browse for the text file you edited in step 4 and then click **Upload**.
9. To view your finished video, click **View on Video Page** located in the top right of the screen.

Some businesses don't like YouTube

Hopefully by now you fully understand the benefits of using such a great video resource to enhance your Prezis. The fact is that YouTube will continue to grow at an incredible rate, and there's no doubt at all that the features mentioned previously will only get better and better with time.

Unfortunately, many large businesses chose to remove access to YouTube for fear of employees wasting time looking at the Ninja Cat or other such videos. This of course will have a huge impact on your Prezi designs, and may even mean that YouTube just isn't an option for you.

If you're lucky though you should be able to convince those important people in your IT departments that when used correctly in Prezi, YouTube can become an extremely powerful business tool.

And don't forget to remind them that any videos you upload can only be viewed by those that see your Prezi because of the Privacy settings we mentioned earlier.

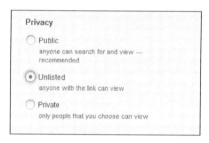

When everything else fails though, fear not. There is still another way.

Windows Live Movie Maker

If you really can't get through to your colleagues in IT to have the YouTube block lifted, then you can still turn to **Windows Live Movie Maker (WLMM)**. We looked at this useful tool a lot in the previous chapter when using audio, but of course, it's real purpose is to work with video. Here we'll look at how to add some of the same effects we saw in the YouTube editing areas.

Make sure that you have Windows Live Movie Maker open on your PC or laptop, and a video file to use.

The Home menu

As soon as you open WLMM, you'll be taken to the home screen. From here, you'll need to load a video by clicking the **Add Videos and Photos** button.

To the right of this button, you can also **Add music** (see *Chapter 2, Using Audio*) and insert a **Title**, **Caption** or **Credits** just as we saw in YouTube.

Clicking on either of these options will create a new screen with different options for text size, background color, and even the start time and text duration.

You can adjust these settings and click on the **Play** button below your movie to see how they look onscreen.

One of the great things about WLMM is that you have the ability to share the video very easily from the home screen. You can see in the following screenshot that there is even an option to upload the video to your YouTube account. This is a huge benefit for those who feel comfortable using WLMM but also want the advantages of having YouTube host the video for you.

There are also lots of different options under the save menu next to the sharing options. For getting video into Prezi, you can select the very first option that says **Recommended for this project** as that will create a .wmv file for you.

Animations menu

If you have created a title screen at the start of your video, then it's important you create a nice transition between that and your video. To do so, simply scroll through and roll over the tiles on the upper-left corner of the screen. Each of these is a different transition that will preview for you before you select it.

The **Pan and zoom** tiles on the upper-right side of the screen will play throughout your video and they too will give you a preview when rolled over with your mouse.

Using these options can help to give your videos a certain style which you may wish to continue if using multiple videos throughout your Prezi.

The Visual Effects menu

Just like we saw in YouTube, the Visual Effects menu has some predefined effects that you can apply to your video. Some of them are pretty crazy, and if you're creating a video for use in a business Prezi, then these might not go down too well with your colleagues in the marketing department.

The most useful option in this menu is the **Brightness** control. Just slide the scale to the right to increase the brightness of the image.

The Edit menu

The Edit menu allows you to fade your audio in and out at the start and end of your movie. This is a really nice feature because it means the person viewing your Prezi won't jump out of their skin as soon as the video starts to play its sound track or the person on the video starts to talk.

The best feature of the Edit screen however is the Trim tool. In YouTube we were only able to trim the start and end of our movie, but in WLMM we can trim any part of the movie, and even trim multiple times if we need to.

1. Click on the **Trim tool** button on the upper-right of the Edit screen.
2. Select one of the video tiles that represent different parts of your video.

3. Then drag the bars just above the play button in the main window to trim out the unwanted parts.

4. Click on **Save trim**.

Inserting WLMM videos into Prezi

Once all your editing and trimming is done, you'll want to finally get your WLMM movie into Prezi. So long as you've saved your movie from the home screen using the **Recommended for this project** option, you won't have any issues at all and your movie will be saved in **Windows Media Video (WMV)** file format.

1. Open Prezi.

2. Go to **Insert** and select **File**.

3. Locate your .wmv movie and click **Open**.

4. If you are using the Prezi desktop application your file will need converting for use in Prezi and an Internet connection will be needed.

5. Once the video is converted, you can edit its position as you would edit any other element on your canvas.

Benefits of Windows Live Movie Maker

One of the key benefits of using WLMM to create videos for Prezi is that you can do everything offline. You don't need to worry about accidentally uploading a video of your companies latest prototype for your competitors to see, and you won't have to try and battle with your IT department to give you access to YouTube.

There are lots of other benefits to using WLMM for videos but there is also one key element that will limit what you can do, and that is file size. The bigger your video files the bigger your Prezi. The bigger the size of your Prezi, the harder it is to transfer onto memory sticks and share over e-mail and so on.

Of course for some of us working in big organizations with solid reliable networks this may not be an issue at all. And of course 2013 is promising to be the era of 4 G. Here's to hoping!

Fun with video in Prezi

So now that you know how to create great looking videos and insert them into Prezi, you might be wondering how you can actually use them in your presentation. Following are just a few suggestions to get you started, but try to think beyond simply inserting video into a presentation. Try and make the use of the video fun and engaging for your audience.

Questions

In most presentations you deliver, there will be some element of quizzing the audience. This should happen throughout so that you can check the audience's understanding of your subject.

Why not use a video clip of a subject matter expert or another colleague other than yourself asking the question, pausing, and then giving a full explanation of the answer.

This will be more visually engaging and will add a really nice touch to your presentation.

Experts

In *Chapter 2*, *Using Audio*, we mentioned using subject matter experts to provide audio content for your Prezi. Of course this goes one step further by using video of them discussing a certain subject.

If they have a good enough web cam, they can easily record a short clip which can be sent to you for editing in either WLMM or YouTube.

Hearing information from experts is a massive benefit for your audience.

Customer scenarios

Most of us have had to be part of some embarrassing role play game during a training session, but a fun way of delivering customer service or soft skills training would be to have a video clip of the customer inserted into your Prezi.

The customer could ask your audience a product-related question, or make a complaint of some kind. Then someone from your audience could deliver a response.

To make it even more fun why not have two alternative videos following on from that – one where the customer is happy with your response and the other where they become slightly more annoyed. Based on the response given from your audience, you can then decide where the Prezi goes next.

Summary

However way you decide to use video in your Prezi, make sure you use the information in this chapter to make your videos look great. As we mentioned at the very start of the chapter a true Prezi Master wouldn't just find a YouTube clip and insert it. They would take some extra time and care to make sure the video at least has a heading. A Prezi Master would also be able to use their own video files and make them look as professional as possible.

Throughout this chapter, we've made the huge benefits very obvious for using either YouTube or Windows Live Movie Maker. Whichever route you decide to take they are bound to give your video files, and ultimately your Prezi, a much bigger impact.

Make sure that you are also aware of the potential pitfalls of both methods as well. To avoid these, you need to know exactly how your Prezi is going to be delivered before you start building it.

The next chapter should really help with this. *Chapter 4, Approaching Your Prezi Design* moves away from the technical elements that have been discussed in previous chapters and focuses on the best way to approach the design of your Prezi.

You will learn a simple three-step process that will help you get the most out of the software and construct new Prezis in a logical fashion.

4
Approaching Your Prezi Design

So far we've looked at the technical elements that can help you master Prezi. Now it's time to look at the process you should use when approaching any Prezi design.

This process will really help you get the most out of Prezi, and more than anything else, it will ensure you construct your Prezi in a very logical and time-efficient manner.

Topics covered in this chapter are:

- Thinking for non-linear presentations
- Mind mapping
- Getting the flavor right
- Building your Prezi in layers
- Knowing your BIG picture

A change of approach

As you have probably figured out by now, Prezi is a completely new way of presenting and is unlike the linear (slide by slide) approach we've all grown used to over the last 100 years or so. Because Prezi is so different both technically and aesthetically, we need to make sure we approach it in a very different way to how we might go about designing a PowerPoint presentation.

It goes without saying that a presentation designed in any media should have a good degree of planning first, but even more so in Prezi. The reason is that Prezi's infinite canvas gives you such a huge expanse of space that it is very easy to lose elements of your design within it.

By simply planning your Prezi in the right way, you can save lots of time in the design stage and really take advantage of this space.

Forget slides

It's easy to keep using the term "slides" when building a Prezi, but slides don't exist in the software and that kind of thinking will keep you stuck in the old way of presenting. Force yourself and your colleagues to use Prezi terms like "canvas" and "frames" to break the mold and get you focused on the right type of approach.

A prison without walls

You probably moved over to Prezi because you were getting tired and fed up with the rigid nature of PowerPoint or some other slide-based tool. You felt trapped and confined by the slides that only allowed you to deliver your presentations in one way: from start to end.

Then you saw Prezi and were blown away by the fact that it is a completely open canvas that doesn't have any walls or restrictions like slides do.

For some though this fact can be very difficult to embrace, and some very quickly return back to the comfort of their slide-walled prisons because too much freedom scares them. They simply don't know how to use the space well to deliver their message. If you watch them closely, you'll see that they are trying to build a slide-show in Prezi and the way they are thinking just doesn't match up with the way Prezi works.

These prisoners could easily be freed by learning how to think and plan for Prezi, and we believe there are three key steps to mastering your Prezi designs which we'll explore later on in the chapter.

No end in sight

If you ask any Prezi master why they love it so much, you might hear the words "non-linear presenting" quite a bit. In order to master Prezi, it's important to know exactly what's meant by a non-linear presentation.

Linear presentations

If we wanted a presentation to show learner drivers how to drive, then we would need to start with the absolute basics and build from there. This type of presentation would have to be linear and might flow something like the following:

1. Unlock the driver's side door.
2. Get in and put your seat belt on.
3. Put your foot down on the clutch to check you are not in gear.
4. Put the keys into the ignition.
5. Start the car.

And so on the instructions would go, so that the task is carried out in the right way. This is a linear path, and any presentation built to visually represent it would have to start at point 1 and then move onto point 2, and so on.

Information of this kind would always need to be presented in a linear fashion so you could use PowerPoint's slide-based design or build a Prezi that uses a series of paths. Both would have clear start and end points.

Non-linear presentations

What if your subject matter had several different areas or modules that didn't have to be presented in a certain order? Who decides where the start and end should be? You? Your manager? The CEO? We'll give you a clue. They're going to be sat right in front of you at your presentation.

One of the main reasons why presentations don't hit the mark is because they don't consider which elements of the content are most important to their audiences. So why not ask them where they'd like to start? Or at least start your presentation with some friendly introductions; start up a conversation and then find out what the most important part of today's topic is to them. If enough people agree on the same area, then zoom straight into that and get going.

This is a non-linear approach to presenting and is extremely easy to implement with Prezi.

The beauty of using this approach in Prezi is that it engages your audience more and lets the conversation you have with them unfolded very naturally. Following is an example template of how you could structure your non-linear presentation to cover five separate modules.

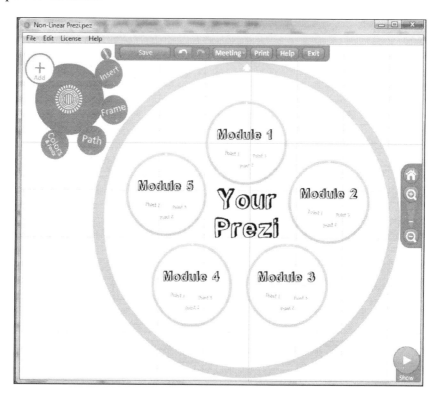

All of the modules are contained inside one giant circular frame, and each module's content is contained inside its own frame within that.

The best of both worlds

Even though a non-linear approach is much more creative, there may be elements to your presentation that are best explained in a linear order for your audience to make sense of them.

If this is the case, you can still join the different elements of your Prezi together with paths. This gives you the benefit of allowing your audience to decide the direction of your presentation (non-linear), but also the opportunity to break down key points into a logical order (linear).

By using Prezis paths tool with this method, your presentation might look as shown in the following screenshot.

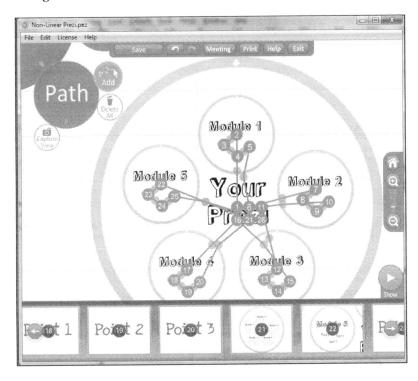

If your audience decides they'd like to start on **Module3**, simply zoom into that frame using your mouse, and then let the paths take over so that you flow through Module 3's content in a linear fashion if needed.

Ask the question

Later in the chapter, we will identify some key questions to help you plan your Prezi. For now though, make sure you always ask the following before you start to build a Prezi.

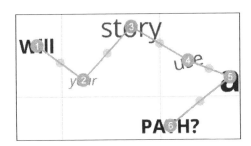

Death by Prezi

It's estimated that nearly 30 million PowerPoint presentations are created every single day. That means there are going to be at least 120 million people sitting through those presentations at some point. And all those millions add up to a lot of lost revenue for businesses across the globe, especially if the audience doesn't retain any of the information due to badly-designed presentations.

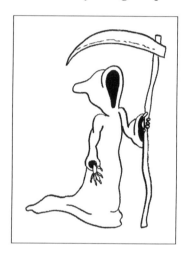

Too much text, five bar charts on the same slide, 20 different types of animations, and the list goes on and on. We're pretty sure you don't need to be told what a bad PowerPoint presentation looks like as most of us have had to sit through hours and hours of them in our careers. What we must try to avoid is a future where the term "death by Prezi" is used just as often as it is today for PowerPoint. So how can we do this and what will absolutely kill a Prezi design?

Think for Prezi

We've already mentioned previously that Prezi can (and should) be used in a non-linear way, but most of us are so used to the linear fashion of PowerPoint and other slide-based tools that we find it very hard to break out of that mold and use this crazy non-linear concept.

By thinking in the old linear slide by slide way, you can end up with what looks like a PowerPoint presentation, but with some fancy transitions in-between slides. If you end up with a presentation like this, then you might as well have continued using PowerPoint because you're not taking full advantage of what Prezi has to offer. Realizing that your presentations movement doesn't just have to go from left (slide 1) to right (slide 2), but that it can also zoom into detail and back out to show an overview of everything, will unlock a whole new world of presentation mastery to you.

There's no doubt that to master Prezi you need to learn two things:

1. The Prezi software
2. The Prezi mindset

Simply knowing what all the buttons do isn't enough to become a Prezi master. You must make sure you take the time to train your brain to think differently as well. Failing to do so will kill a Prezi design.

 Step 1 in the Prezi design approach will help you think in the right way for Prezi.

Motion sickness

One of the biggest attractions to Prezi is the zooming and spinning that happens when transitioning from one element to another. This movement is so smooth and fluent that it's normally the first thing to make people sit up straight and say "Wow this is great, how do you do that?"

The danger with this is that people then go off and create their own Prezi with as many spins and zooms as they can because they think it looks so great that their presentation is bound to be talked about for ages by their colleagues.

Their Prezi will only be talked about for one reason, and that's because after 20 minutes of all the spinning and zooming people had to leave the room because they felt ill.

The spins and zooms you can create in Prezi can be very useful in helping you tell your story, especially if used cleverly by slowly revealing words or zooming in to find hidden details. On their own, they have no impact at all and do not help your audience retain any information.

 Don't rely on the zoom to tell your story. You, your content and some subtle clever use of Prezi will do that, not a 360 degree rotation between each key point!

Master the approach

If your boss asks you to build a presentation on that new business idea you mentioned to them at the Christmas party, you're bound to get very excited indeed. Then they ask if you could present the idea to the board in an hour's time and you slowly start to melt in your chair!

Most people would grab a strong coffee, open up their copy of Prezi and start to insert images, text, video, and anything else they can find to help explain their idea. They would then link the key elements together with paths and be happy that they're Prezi will really communicate their idea enough to get a good result.

A Prezi master on the other hand wouldn't even dream of touching the Prezi software until they knew exactly how their Prezi was going to deliver their idea, which imagery to use, and what the key messages are. In fact, if they had one hour to build a Prezi, they would probably spend the first 15-20 minutes planning and the rest of the time actually building their Prezi. This is because they've taken the time to learn the three design steps to building a Prezi presentation.

One of these employees will get booted out of the boardroom for giving their senior management team motion sickness, and the other gets commended for delivering a wonderfully clear picture of their business idea. We're pretty sure you know which is which.

 Make sure you master the design steps explained next. It is one thing to know the software, but to build really great presentations, you must go about the design in the right way.

The three Prezi design steps

The three-step approach explained over the next few pages is aimed at helping you get the most out of Prezi. By making sure you follow the three steps, you'll start to think in the right way, understand the key messages in your design, and also build the Prezi in a sensible and time-efficient way.

The three steps are:

1. Plan your Prezi.
2. Get the flavor right.
3. Build in layers.

Failure to use this approach can mean you get frustrated in your design and lose track of everything on your canvas, waste valuable time, and/or you end up creating something that's sure to deliver motion sickness to your audience.

To master Prezi, you must master these steps.

Step 1 – Plan your Prezi

The first design step is without a doubt the most important of all. Taking the time to plan your Prezi will give you a clear vision of exactly what it is that you need to say or show to your audience in order to deliver your message.

Things you need to know

There are some questions you should always ask yourself at the start of any Prezi design:

1. What's the overall message I'm trying to get across?
2. What must people know by the end of my Prezi?
3. Are there any smaller key messages along the way that will help to make my point?
4. Will my Prezi be presenter led, or will it be accessed by people online?

Answering these questions before you start can give you a really good understanding of what your Prezi needs to say and how it can be said.

Mind Mapping

You may be familiar with the term Mind Mapping, and if not, we'd definitely recommend you look it up to help with this first Prezi design step. We'll explain it in the following screenshot in more detail, but it's definitely a subject that Prezi masters will want to explore more in their own time.

In essence, Mind Mapping is a way of spreading your ideas out onto a piece of paper or any canvas available instead of just writing a very dull (and linear) list of what's needed in your Prezi presentation. You can see a very simple example of Mind Mapping in the following diagram which we created to help us understand how to best communicate the three Prezi design steps in this chapter.

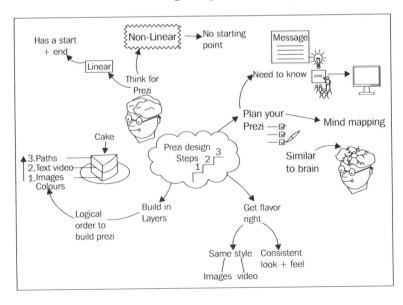

You can see that this Mind Map uses words and pictures to make associations. This is extremely important when planning a Prezi because the more visual, the better it is for your audience.

Why not just write a list?

If you aren't used to using the Mind Mapping technique, it can be a little hard to understand why you should start now and not just write a list of what needs to go into your Prezi.

We've already mentioned that Prezi is a non-linear presentation tool, so it makes perfect sense that you should plan your Prezi in a non-linear way. Forcing yourself to plan in this way and spread your ideas out onto one page will start to give you a great idea of how your Prezi will look because Prezi itself is one giant canvas.

Writing a list to plan your Prezi will encourage you to construct it in a very linear fashion like you would construct a PowerPoint presentation.

How to do it?

Mind Mapping is an amazing tool for generating and planning ideas, but it does take practice. If you haven't done it before, then start now by following the instructions given:

1. Grab a pen and paper and start by writing the subject of your Prezi in the center of your page, that is, **My business**.

2. Circle the title and link any sub headings or important subjects that spring to mind around it with arrows. These could be your company departments or products.

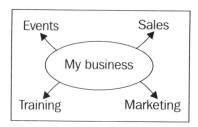

3. Then focus on one sub heading at a time and write any key information you can think of around that. Again link each point back to its heading with arrows or lines.

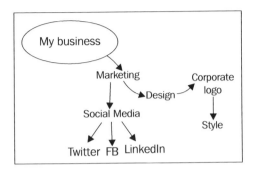

4. Keep repeating these steps until you have either ran out of things to write, or you've found the key points to explain in your Prezi.

[Try to avoid using ruled paper as it may encourage you to start writing a list instead of a Mind Map.]

5. Once you identify the key points that need to be presented in your Prezi, underline them or highlight them in some way so that they stand out from everything else.

6. For each of the key points, try to think of an image that will help visualize it and do a quick sketch of the image. It doesn't have to be a work of art!

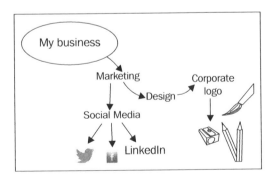

If you aren't familiar with the Mind Mapping technique, then try to go through the preceding steps as many times as you can, and for as many subjects as you can think of.

This form of mental exercise will help you think in the right way for Prezi, and will also help your brain make connections between the text and imagery on your map.

Why it works well with Prezi?

We've already mentioned that Mind Mapping is great for planning Prezis because they both use a canvas in the same way. But there is another more scientific explanation as to why this technique and Prezi work so well in communicating ideas.

It's to do with the way that our brains retain information. And while the inner workings of the human brain aren't yet fully understood, we do know that ideas form when the brain creates neural networks between the vast amounts of information that goes into our heads every day.

When presenting to an audience the best way to get them to remember something is to zoom in on individual details one at a time, then try to show them some kind of link between these details, or at least show them all of the details in one single view and frame them for our audience.

This simple trick is called the BIG picture technique and is explained further on in this chapter. It is simply a way of allowing your audiences brains to connect the dots and retain the information you want them too.

Map your journey

Make sure that you spend enough time as is needed to fully plan out your Prezi in a Mind Map. Some people will find this very easy and natural to do, while others may struggle to think in this way. Whichever end of the spectrum you fall into, make sure you keep doing it and never approach the Prezi software until you have your map in front of you.

By doing this, you'll know:

- What your key points are
- What images you need to tell the story
- How big your Prezi might be
- Where you will need to zoom in to explain details
- What could visually link everything together (your BIG picture)

Change your mind

To help you perfect the art of Mind Mapping, try to use it to plan other things in your work and life, not just your Prezi designs. It is such a powerful tool and can really help you explore possibilities in any area that you decide needs a little focus.

Step 2 – Get the flavor right

Have you ever been in a presentation and spent too much time trying to figure out what the image is onscreen rather than what the actual message from the presenter is? Anything visual in your presentation can be extremely powerful for the audience, or it can be extremely distracting and cloud the importance of your message.

With Prezi's zooming function, you have the power to really deliver a strong message to your audience. With great power comes great responsibility and you must make sure you don't kill your presentation and distract your audience.

To achieve this, you have to think about the style and flavor of your Prezi. Even if you don't have a single creative bone in your body, there are a few things you absolutely must try and achieve, and a few things you should definitely avoid.

What's wrong with this picture?

Image 1   Image 2   Image 3

Let's say that a presentation to new recruits of your smoothie-making company used the three images shown in the preceding screenshot all at the same time in one single frame to explain how a strawberry smoothie should be made.

Any ordinary Prezi user would say that's fine. It clearly shows some nice tasty strawberries. A Prezi master however would not be satisfied with these images together for the reasons we hope you'll spot in the following screenshot.

Image 1   Image 2   Image 3
Vector image   *Clip art*   *Raster image*

Just in case you haven't spotted what's wrong with this image yet, it's down to the fact that the three images are all different styles and formats.

Image 1 is a vector which is in either PDF or SWF format (perfect for zooming). Image 2 is a raster clip art and image 3 is a raster image as well. We explored the differences between raster and vector images in *Chapter 1, Best Practices with Imagery* and you should know that while they both have their pros and cons, you should try and avoid using both at the same time, and especially in the same frame.

These are clearly all strawberries, but they are all of a different flavor!

Consistency

Try to use imagery that has the same look and style by using the same online library to purchase the images. Alternatively, just spend a little more time searching in Google for images that look right together. If you decide to vectorise one image (as explained in *Chapter 1, Best Practices with Imagery*), then make sure you do the same for all images to get the same style. This will also make your Prezi much smaller in file size.

Frame it right

A useful tip to help you get a consistent flavor throughout your Prezi is to create a series of frames with text and image placeholders inside them to use as templates. This is much like creating a slide master in PowerPoint so that each time you move to a different section of your Prezi the information can be displayed in a consistent way.

As this isn't yet a feature of the Prezi software, the best way to create these templates is to go to a blank space on your canvas and place a frame there. Enter some text inside the frame and call it templates so you don't forget what it's for.

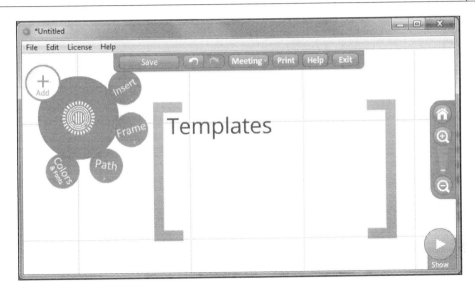

Inside this new frame, create your frame templates to use throughout your Prezi. They can be as detailed or as simple as you like, and remember because Prezi zooms, you will be able to place these templates inside one another in your design.

Use Prezis rectangle shapes tool to indicate where images should be positioned, and simple text fields where information can be entered. The following examples are very simple, but hopefully give you the right idea.

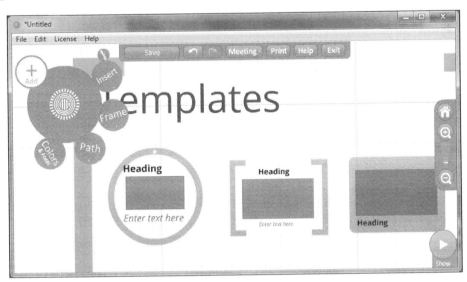

Once you have these frame templates in place, you can move to this area of your canvas at any time to copy one of them and then paste it into the position that is required in your design.

 The **Prezis+** button from the bubble menu will allow you to add frames and text together, but it is very limited and does not allow for customization of frames as described previously.

Themes

In business presentations, it's easy to get carried away and disregard the corporate color scheme that your marketing department spent so long developing. The result could be a presentation that doesn't look connected to your business at all.

Make sure you don't upset your coloring department and stick to the company color theme by using the Prezi **Colors and Fonts** feature from the bubble menu.

From this menu, you can access **Theme Wizard** and duplicate your company's corporate style. In order to get the colors exactly right, click on the **Manual** button in the bottom left of the **Theme Wizard**.

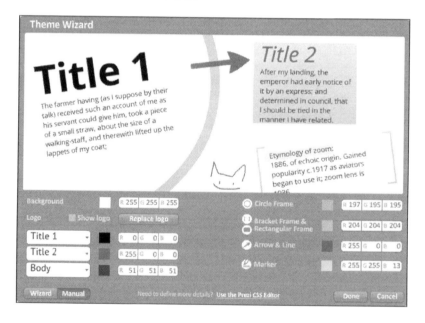

You will need to know the RGB (Red Green Blue) values of your company's color theme to enter them in the fields shown in the preceding screenshot. In the preceding screenshot, you can also add your company logo.

Company template

To save time in future Prezi designs create a blank Prezi file that has the correct color theme and logo. Make sure you have some frame templates to use somewhere on the Prezi canvas as well. Then save the Prezi as "company template" to be used as a starting point for every new design.

Step 3 – Building in layers

Now comes the easy part! Taking the Prezi design, you've mind mapped in step 1, added all of the imagery and styles from step 2, and put it all together on the Prezi canvas. It's a piece of cake right?

We're pretty sure that every Prezi user comes unstuck now and again because they rush into the canvas and try to add everything at once. This can lead to certain elements getting lost because you zoomed in too far and then back out again, or you might find that your Prezi doesn't end up looking like you imagined from the Mind Map in step 1.

Piece of cake

In order to help you in this final step, we want you to think of making your Prezi in the same way that you'd make a delicious Victoria sponge cake like the one in the following image.

Once you've got all of your ingredients from steps 1 and 2, you should build your Prezi in the layers listed as follows.

Bottom layer of sponge

If you're going to have some kind of background image that sits behind everything in your Prezi, then you must insert this onto your canvas before anything else. It may be that you want to start your Prezi by zooming into a small part of a much larger image which will be revealed at the end. In which case, make sure it's the first thing you insert.

In the example shown in the following image, the Prezi starts in the top left of the iPad screen at path points 1 and 2. The audience is then taken through the Prezi path which is all contained inside the screen of the iPad. It is only when the audience reaches path point 12 that the Prezi zooms out to reveal the background image.

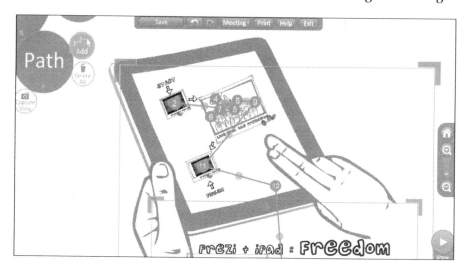

This example can be viewed online at `http://prezi.com/yl9_u5si57pp/prezi-ipad-freedom/`.

 The technique of revealing an eye-catching background image at the end of your Prezi is known as the Big picture technique and is explained a little more at the end of this chapter.

If you aren't inserting a background image, then you might still want to have a background color so make sure you spend some time in the **Theme Wizard** area mentioned earlier to get this right.

Cream and Jam

Now that you have your first layer of sponge in place, you can start to add those tasty ingredients and spread them right across your Prezi canvas. Yummy!

The cream and jam of your Prezi might include some or all of the following items:

- Text
- Images
- Graphs
- Video files (including sound)
- YouTube clips
- Flash animations
- Frames

If you've planned your Prezi well enough in step 1, then you should have a good idea of where to place each of these elements on your canvas.

Remember how easy it is to give your audience motion sickness, so try not to space the elements out too far from one another. The transition from one key point to the other could happen at lightning speed if they are positioned a mile apart.

We'd also encourage you to place the separate elements at slightly different angles from one another so that the canvas turns a little during transition. But again try not to overcook this as too much spinning will make people feel ill.

If you do need to adjust the position of any object in this stage, just right-click it and use the **Send Backward** or **Bring Forward** options as shown in the following screenshot.

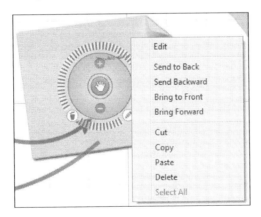

Top layer of sponge

Once you have your background imagery (bottom layer) and your different elements (cream and jam) on the same canvas, the only thing left to do is join them all together with paths so that your Prezi flows in the correct order.

 As we've already mentioned, your Prezi design might not need a path. So for some, this step might be optional.

It can be extremely difficult and frustrating to try to adjust paths when things need to be moved around on your canvas, so make sure you are totally happy with the position of your cream and jam before adding this top layer of sponge.

Once you've added your paths, we strongly recommend you take your Prezi into show mode and test that everything looks and tastes great.

The steps, again

We highly recommend that you master these three design steps as they will really help you achieve great results and visualize the design before you even touch the Prezi software.

Knowing what you want to achieve from your Prezi at the start is crucial. It's extremely easy to get lost in the Prezi canvas and waste time looking for missing objects, so adding this very structured and logical approach will really help.

As a reminder the three Prezi design steps are:

1. Plan your Prezi.
2. Get the flavor right.
3. Build in layers.

Once you master these steps building any Prezi will be a piece of cake.

Don't get caught out!

When building a Prezi for your business, you'll no doubt be under serious time restraints, have other work that needs your attention, and probably have a number of distractions around you. Don't allow yourself to skip over these steps because you think there isn't time. Avoid a "death by Prezi" future in your business and stay focused on the steps. They"ll save you time if used correctly.

Presenting your BIG picture

Throughout this chapter we've mentioned a concept called the BIG picture, so now it's time to explain it in more detail and give you the tools to master this great technique. By taking all of the skills you've learned so far and combining them with a great way of delivering your Prezi, you're bound to be viewed as a Prezi master by colleagues and bosses alike.

The BIG picture technique is a way of presenting your information to an audience so that they can understand how different elements link together. It enables you to structure your message in a way that will be more memorable to your audience, giving your business Prezis a much higher impact than the traditional presenting tools.

The science behind it

The brain is made up of tiny nerve cells called neurons, these neurons have tiny branch-like structures that reach out and connect with other neurons. Each place where a neuron connects with another neuron is called a synapse or synaptic connection. The pattern and way our neurons connect to each other forms our neural network. These networks form our ideas, thoughts, and memories.

Think of these neural networks in the same way as the mind maps we looked at earlier. Our brains take in thousands of tiny stimuli every second. In a presentation, the stimuli would normally be images, words and sounds from the presenter and the group we might be sitting with. Our brains take everything in and connect the dots with neural networks between each piece of stimuli. Where a connection is made, an idea is formed.

In the traditional slide by slide approach to presenting, it is more difficult for the brain to make connections. This is generally a downside to the way presentations are put together, that is, it's hard to connect a concept on slide 2 to something on slide 50 an hour later!

Because Prezi gives us such freedom to move around the canvas and zoom in and out of different elements, it's very easy for us to present in a way that aids the brain in creating neural networks. This, in turn, leads to our Prezis messages being remembered for longer and in more detail than by using slides.

Neural networks in action

In order to explain how Prezi can help build neural networks what better tool to use than Prezi itself? If you have an Internet connection while you're reading this, you can go to `http://prezi.com/vuf5fbirwjke/big-picture-thinking/` and see a Prezi explaining this concept. If you don't have an Internet connection, we've added screenshots of the same Prezi.

If you follow the steps explained as follows when constructing your Prezi, you are bound to deliver a much more powerful message.

1. Show your audience the first piece of information

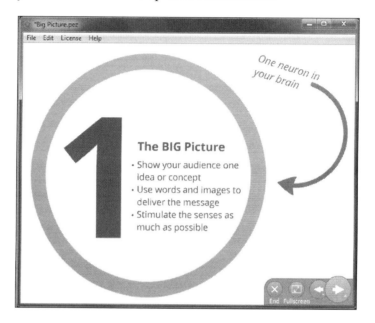

2. Move to the next piece of information and don't rush things.

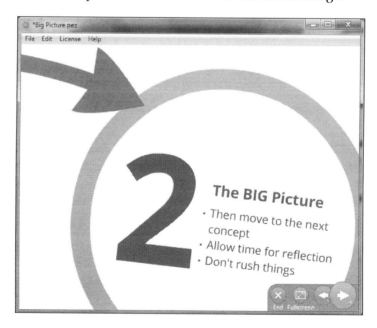

3. Move along again until you've covered all the key elements.

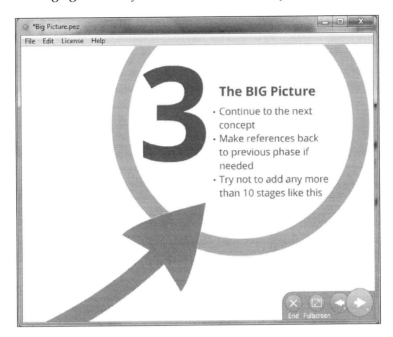

4. Zoom out to show all of the key elements and their relationships in one view.

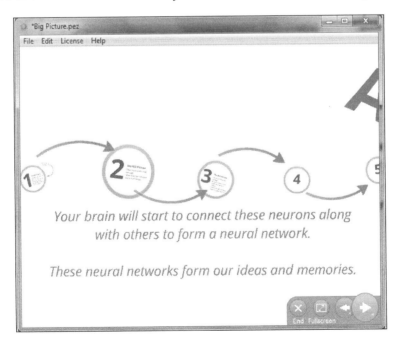

5. You can even zoom out again to display even more relationships between information.

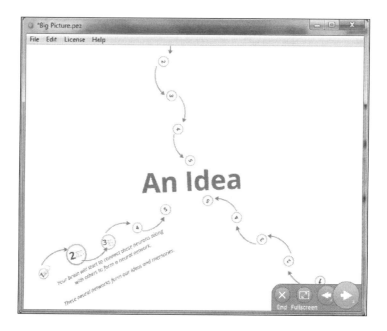

6. Your audience will remember the relationships and understand the BIG picture.

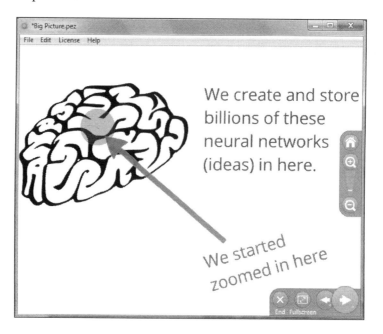

You can create a copy of the above Prezi online at `http://prezi.com/vuf5fbirwjke/big-picture-thinking/` to store in your own Prezi account.

This Prezi explains how to help create the neural networks discussed by using the BIG picture technique itself.

You can see how at the start we are already zoomed into one neuron of the brain, and then we slowly move outwards. The fourth and fifth images clearly show the connections between everything we've previously seen in the Prezi.

In the final frame of the Prezi, we zoom out completely to see an image of the brain. This is the BIG picture view for this particular Prezi as it clearly demonstrates that everything we've been seeing happens inside the human brain.

If you can deliver every message in your presentation in this way, then you truly will be a Prezi master.

How to find your BIG picture

If done correctly, you should start to see your BIG picture form in the planning stage of your Prezi (step 1 of any Prezi design). By using the Mind Mapping techniques explained earlier, you will start to see connections between the different elements of your Prezi. At this stage you should ask yourself the question "What single image could sum up the links between everything?"

It might be difficult to find the right image, and in some cases it might need a combination of images together. But the key messages along the way should all be delivered inside of the BIG picture.

BIG picture in reverse

You can also try using the BIG picture technique in reverse order. Show the BIG picture at the very start of your Prezi, then zoom into the details and explain the relationships.

To help you practice finding images that sum up a series of different elements and link them together, have a go at completing the following table. Hopefully you'll start to get much better at this with time – and if you master the three Prezi design steps of course!

				What image would you use to connect everything?
Book	Cream	Glasses	Towel	
Mushrooms	Dough	Tomatoes	Cheese	
Club	Tee	Ball	Sand	

Summary

This chapter has given a chance to master the non-technical element of Prezi. This is an element of the software that is either forgotten or just not given any thought at all by most Prezi users. However, it is just as important as learning what each button does inside the software itself and some people would even argue that it's more important than knowing the software.

It's one thing to know how to drive a car, but if you don't know how to drive it sensibly and think about other road users, then you are sure to crash eventually and really hurt someone. Make sure you master the techniques in this chapter and align the way you think and plan a presentation to the way that Prezi works. By doing this, you will cruise down the highway looking like a total super star to everyone in your business.

In the next chapter, we're back to the technical side of Prezi with a look at using projectors to present. Although a fairly simple subject, there are some key points to be aware of, and also some very clever stuff to be learned for those real masters willing to put in the extra effort.

5

Projecting Your Prezi

This chapter looks at some technical aspects you should be aware of when using a projector to show off your Prezi. Although a very simple subject, there are some important things to point out that could interfere with your design.

We'll also introduce you to an exciting new concept that, with a small amount of time and investment, is sure to wow your audience and really open your eyes to a new way of delivering.

Topics to be covered are:

- A common mistake
- Aspect ratios
- The best way to insert frames
- Sharing Prezis for others to present
- Creating an interactive whiteboard

Planning your Prezi

In the previous chapter, we talked about the three Prezi design steps, and hopefully by now you realize the importance of planning your Prezi. If you don't, then stop right here and go back to *Chapter 4, Approaching Your Prezi Design!*

One of the questions you needed to know the answer to in the planning stage was:

Will my Prezi be presenter led, or will it be accessed by people online?

We'll cover the approach needed when designing Prezis for online use in the next chapter, but for now, let's imagine your Prezi is going to be presenter led. Chances are that this will be true for the vast majority of Prezis within your business anyway, so it makes sense to tackle this subject first.

A common mistake

Before we go into any real detail on the subject of projectors, it's important that we explain a simple concept that most of us struggle with initially in Prezi. Thankfully there's also a simple solution as well, so read on.

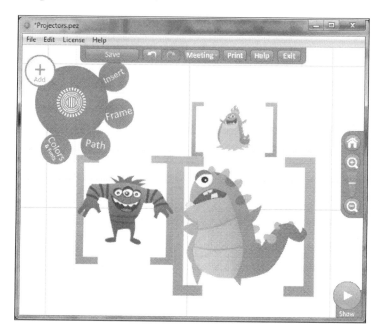

Let us imagine we've just designed the Prezi as shown in the preceding screenshot. We want to introduce our audience to the three characters one at a time. We've linked the frames, containing each character with a path and we want each one to fill the screen that were projecting onto.

What do you think will happen when we go into show mode and click through the paths? Let's take a look and see:

1. Path point 1 – What's that orange blob on the right?

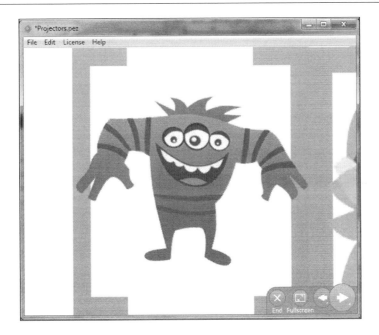

2. Path point 2 - Looks okay but there's a lot of empty space above and below the frame.

3. Path point 3 – Who's arm is that in my view?

You can see in the preceding screenshot that as the paths move to each frame we can see parts of the other frames around them. Path point 3 is the best example as you can see the arm of the purple character creeping into the left of the screen. This can cause a lot of frustration, and if there are even more objects in your design, it can be very distracting for the audience. Some will lose focus, and others may sit there thinking "What is that on the side of the screen?" while you try to deliver an important message!

So what's happening here? Hopefully the Prezi Master in you spotted the cause of all this trouble. If not, then take another look at the following screenshot which shows all of the frames together.

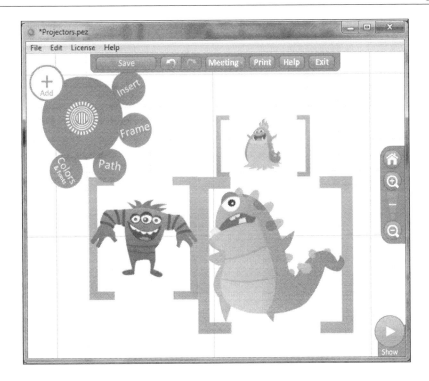

Figured it out yet?

Okay, we'll put you out of your misery. Look at the size and shape of the frames. The bottom two frames in particular are almost perfect squares. Is your PC or Mac screen square? No.

If we're telling our Prezis path to link to a square frame, then that's what it will do. It will place this square frame in the center of your rectangular screen or wherever you're projecting. It, therefore, stands to reason that anything else around the square frame is going to show up around the edges.

The simple solution

This problem will have started when you dragged your frames onto the canvas.

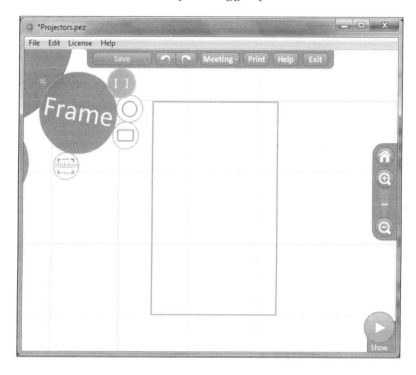

You can see in the preceding screenshot that a frame is being dragged onto the canvas in a tall rectangular shape. You can create frames of any shape or length that you like, but if you do, you'll end up in the same mess we explained previously.

The simple solution is to hold down the *Shift* key on your keyboard as you drag your new frame onto the canvas. By doing this your frame will be set to a ratio of 4:3 and should be the same shape as the following screenshot. We'll explain what the 4:3 ratio means later in this chapter.

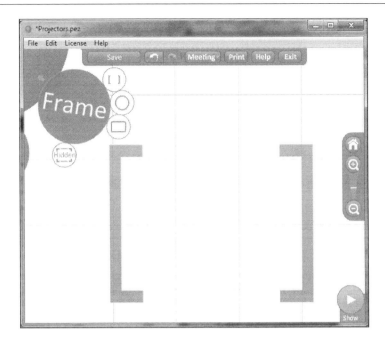

Master's secret shortcut

A very useful (but not well known) shortcut that helps when designing for use on projectors is to hold down the *Ctrl* + *Shift* + *M* keys on your keyboard. Doing so will allow you to see a grid in the center of your screen which is perfectly sized for the 4:3 ratio we discussed previously.

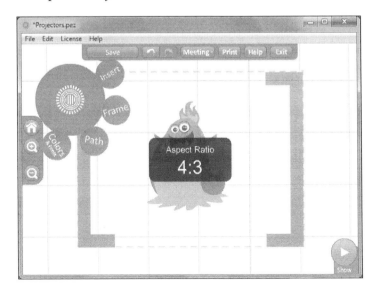

In the preceding screenshot you can see there is a grid with a broken line in the center of the screen. The frame we've added to our Prezi fits perfectly inside this grid which means it will display perfectly on a 4:3 aspect ratio projector (the standard).

Pressing the *Ctrl + Shift + M* keys again will switch the grid to a 16:9 aspect ratio. You can see this in the following screenshot with the same frame we looked at a moment ago. Now the grid in the center of the screen is a lot wider and shorter.

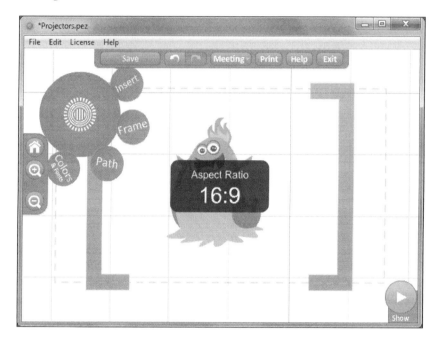

If you're using a projector or screen that operates at the 16:9 ratio, then your frames and content need to fit inside the grid.

Pressing the *Ctrl + Shift + M* keys again will switch off the grid view.

 If you're certain your Prezi will be projected, then use the *Ctrl + Shift + M* shortcut as soon as you create the new Prezi file.

Why you need to know about ratios?

Nowadays, most PCs and Laptops are widescreen. But the majority of projectors on the market have an aspect ratio of 4:3. The term aspect ratio refers to the ratio of a picture's width to its height. If the aspect ratio of a picture were 1:1, the width and height would be the same, and you'd have a perfect square.

The aspect ratio of 4:3 means for every four units of width, the picture will be three units high as shown in the following screenshot.

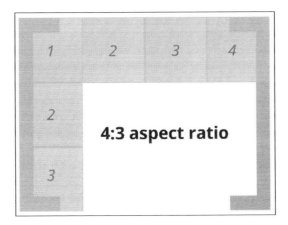

What this means for your Prezi

Essentially what's happening here is that most of us are designing our Prezis on a screen that is much wider than the projector being used in the end result. What happens then is that our Prezis end up with lots of empty space in each frame or elements from other frames creeping into view because the frame isn't the right size.

The following screenshot is an example of a Prezi being designed on a widescreen laptop. It's a very common mistake to try and fill the screen with content and to then insert a frame around everything that fills the screen.

This may look fine when on a laptop screen, but when projecting at a ratio of 4:3, as shown in the following screenshot, you can see that the frame does not fill the screen and there is a lot of space wasted above and below.

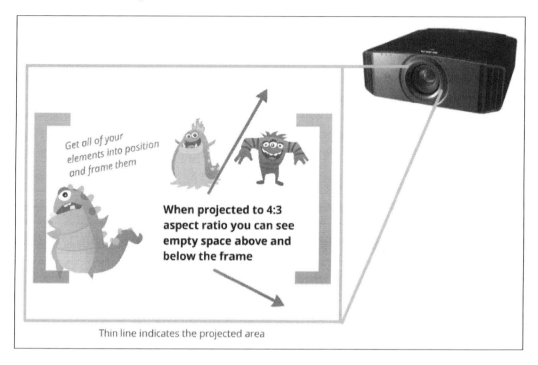

As we saw earlier in this chapter, a big annoyance might be that the space around your frame contains other elements which shouldn't be in this view. That will be very distracting to your audience, and if you're trying to use the BIG picture method it could actually give the game away to early.

Build your Prezi at the 4:3 ratio

As we explained earlier, to keep your Prezi looking exactly the same on your laptop as it does when projected, you must hold down the *Shift* key when inserting a frame.

By doing this, the frame will automatically size itself to the 4:3 ratio and you won't be disappointed by things looking different when projected. Follow these steps and projectors won't trouble you anymore:

1. Decide where your frame should go and move to that area of the canvas.

2. Click on **Frames** and select any of the frame types you'd like to use.

3. Hold down the *Shift* key on your keyboard.

4. Click onto your canvas and drag across to create your frame.

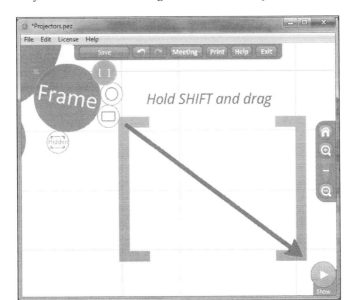

You'll notice the shape of the frame will stay the same as you create it. This is the 4:3 ratio taking effect because you have the *Shift* key held down.

5. Release the mouse button before the *Shift* key to make sure the ratio stays at 4:3.

6. Now place your content inside the frame and continue with your design.

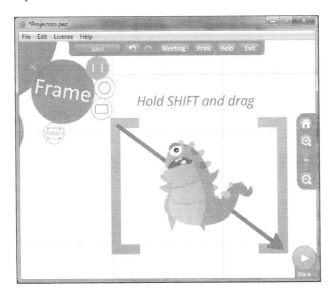

[Circular frames do not conform to ratios simply because of their shape.]

Hopefully you have a much clearer idea now as to why this problem might have crept into your designs in the past. The following image illustrates the difference that holding down the *Shift* key will make to your presentation. The numbered grey squares indicate the 4:3 ratio that will appear in the projection. You can see that the frame on the right will have most of its content missing once projected.

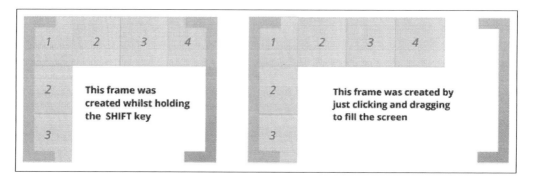

Beware the double-click!

We just wanted to make you aware of something that happens too often, and is a really easy mistake to make. Sometimes you can do it without knowing and end up changing your frame size.

As you may be aware by now, you can double-click most objects inserted into Prezi in order to edit them. When you double-click a frame, you can change its size and dimensions by dragging the corners as shown in the following screenshot.

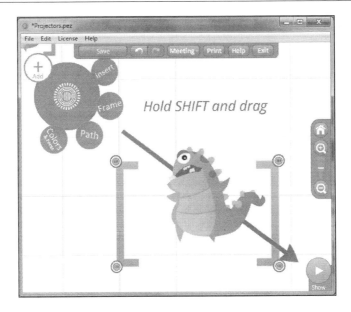

Unfortunately, when you edit a frame in this way, the *Shift* key will not register with Prezi and your frame will no longer be set to 4:3 ratio. Ouch!

If you do need to change the size or position of your frame, we strongly recommend you click the frame and then use the transformation zebra as shown in the following screenshot.

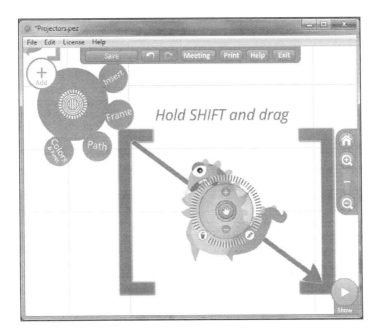

When positioning all your objects onto the canvas, it's very easy to double-click a frame and accidently resize it. Just press *Ctrl+Z* on your keyboard to undo the change.

Sharing your Prezi

If you're building a Prezi for someone else in your organization, it might be safer (for you and them) to export your design as a portable Prezi. This means that they won't be able to edit the Prezi file at all, but they also won't need to have Prezi installed on their computer to present it.

For Prezi desktop users, follow the given steps to export your work as a portable Prezi:

1. Click on the **File** menu at the top of the screen.
2. Select the option **Export as portable prezi...**
3. Name the file and click on the **Save** button.

For Prezi online users, follow the given steps to export your work as a portable Prezi:

1. Exit the Prezi canvas to go back to your Prezis info page.

2. Below the preview window, click on the **Download** button.

3. Select the option **Export to portable prezi...**

4 Click on the **Download** button and wait a few seconds.

5. You will then see the message **Your downloadable prezi has been created. Please click this link to download the file**.

6. Click the link and decide the location for the file to be saved on your computer.

In both cases, what you will end up with is a compressed (zipped) folder containing an executable (.exe) file called **prezi**. This file is your Prezi design and simply double-clicking it will allow it to play on any PC or Mac without an Internet connection.

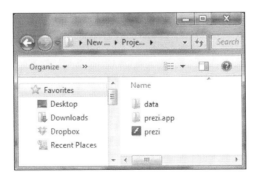

The **data** and **prezi.app** folders must be kept with the **prezi** file as they contain content items that the file needs to function properly.

It's definitely worth dropping a note to whomever will be presenting the Prezi that it must not be removed from the main project folder.

 Remember that if you have any YouTube clips in your Prezi then you will need an Internet connection to play them.

Interactive Prezis

In the previous chapter, we talked about how Prezi presentations can be non-linear. And how the information and order in which you present can be led by the audience rather than someone following a rigid script. Well, what if we could take that concept one step further and actually put the presentation into the hands of our audience for them to explore?

What if we created a presentation that the audience could explore on an **Interactive Whiteboard (IWB)** that is being projected onto a wall or desk in front of them? You, as the presenter, could simply facilitate their exploration, show them how to use the tools, and of course, help them out if they got stuck. Wouldn't that increase the engagement levels even more?

If you like the sound of that but are thinking "Wait, there's no way I can get sign off to buy an IWB" don't panic because there is a way to create your own IWB that you can carry around in your bag, that costs less than $200, and works great with Prezi.

All you need are the following items to get you started:

- Standard projector
- Smoothboard IWB software installed on your PC or MAC. Can be purchased from http://www.smoothboard.net for less than $30
- Infrared pen
- Nintendo wii remote
- USB Bluetooth module, to link the wii remote to your PC. (If your PC has built-in Bluetooth, you won't need to purchase this)

How it works

The full user guide for the Smoothboard IWB software can be found here at http://www.smoothboard.org/manual. For detailed information on the software, visit the site. We'll aim to give you a simple explanation of how it works, and of course, we'll give you some ideas on how it might be used to create some exciting Prezis.

Once the Smoothboard software is installed onto your PC, you can access a feature called **SmoothConnect**. This feature will automatically detect any wii remotes that are turned on nearby.

 You will need a Bluetooth-enabled PC or a USB Bluetooth module in order to connect the wii remote to your PC via SmoothConnect

Once the wii remote is connected to Smoothboard, you can position it on your desk so that it is facing toward the same area you are projecting your Prezi canvas onto.

The infrared pens transmit a signal whenever they are pressed. If the wii remote picks up an infrared signal in the area being projected, it will behave the same as if you were clicking on the Prezi canvas. This means you can click and drag the canvas in any direction, or click on frames to zoom in on certain details and objects.

The following image shows you how all of the different items work together to create the IWB.

 The wii remote can be placed anywhere in the room, but must be pointing at the projected area in order to create the IWB effect.

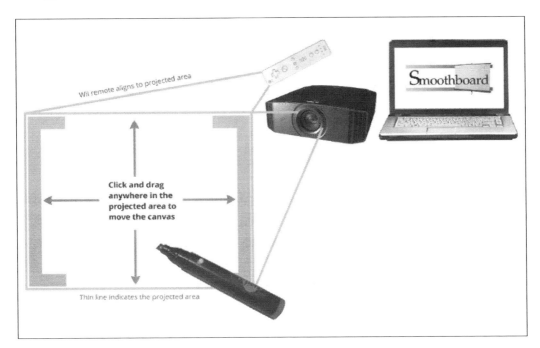

How will you use it

You might not want to use this method for all your presentations, but it can certainly add more interaction than the standard way we deliver information. We hope you can come up with some really creative uses for Prezis being displayed with an IWB, but here are some tips to help you make the most of it.

- Give instructions
    - Some people fear technology. To make sure your session is highly interactive, start explaining how the system works within five minutes or so. You don't want to scare people off before you've even gotten started, so let everyone have a chance to use the pens and drag the canvas around.
    - It might be a good idea to create an individual Prezi that has instructions all over it for people to follow. Once you and your audience feel confident enough then get started.

- Carry a spare!
    - If you're planning on using this system for a whole day, then make sure you have some spare batteries for your wii remote and infrared pens. Nothing is more annoying than when you've told everyone to expect something amazing, and then it doesn't work!

- Try using more pens
    - You don't just have to use one pen in your presentation. You might want to split the audience into groups and give them a pen each. Then, when it's their turn to interact with the canvas, they take control.

> Note that using two pens does not give you the pinch and zoom effect that we're all so used to on smart phones and tablets.

- Project onto a desk
    - If you want to get a little more creative and really make your presentation a memorable one, then why not try projecting onto something other than a wall or white screen. If you have a board room with a decent size desk, then you could project onto that and create an interactive surface there instead.

- You'll need to make sure you can place your projector and wii remote high enough above the desk so that your Prezi fills the available area. You can do this safely by using a projector stand, extending it as high as it will go, and pointing it down at the desk.

- You may need to adjust the keystone settings on your projector so that you get the same rectangular shape as the desk. Accessing these settings will be different on every projector, but normally accessed via the menu button on the projector itself.

- Use the space

  - You want to make this as engaging as possible for people, so use a lot more space in-between frames and areas of content than you would normally use. This means the audience will have to physically drag the canvas a lot more to find different areas of your design. People learn from experiences more than anything else, so make it fun and make sure they are all on their feet exploring the canvas.

Summary

As you can see from the topics covered in this chapter, the way in which you project your Prezi can add so much more to the impact of your presentation. It's an area that is often overlooked and not given much thought to because we've become so used to just plugging projectors into our laptops and using the cleanest wall space available.

Make sure that you give this area some thought in the planning stage of your Prezi. If you know which projector is to be used in your organization, then check to see if it does use a 4:3 ratio. If your Prezi is going to get passed around and used on multiple projectors and screens, then stick to the 4:3 ratio in your design to be safe.

For those truly dedicated to becoming a Prezi master, invest some time (and a little money) in setting up your own IWB. Design a Prezi that allows your audience to explore and interact with your Prezi. Sit back and revel in your greatness.

In the next chapter, we will look at designing a Prezi that will be accessed by people online. You'll need to take a slightly different approach and think about your audience a lot more. People have a very short attention span when working online so this chapter will help you engage with them and keep them focused by using some added extras in your design.

6
Prezis for Online Delivery

When you first discovered Prezi, you probably spent a long time on the **Explore** page of www.prezi.com looking at other people's designs. Most of the Prezis you'll come across on the explore page have been designed for delivery by a presenter so they sometimes don't make sense, or there just isn't enough text or video to understand the points trying to be made.

One of the amazing things about Prezi is that it's so easy to share your presentations with colleagues in your organization; and even with the rest of the world, if you chose too. But what's the point of doing this if your Prezi hasn't been designed with online viewing in mind? Will your colleagues be amazed by the spinning and zooming, but not realize what the message is that you're trying to get across?

There are a number of business reasons why designing a Prezi for people to explore online is more beneficial than delivering it face to face. This chapter sheds some light on how best to approach the design of Prezis for online delivery and covers the following areas:

- Your Prezis
  - Privacy settings
  - Search engines

- Sharing a Prezi
  - Embedding a Prezi into your website
- Approaching your design
- Design tips for online Prezis

Your Prezis

From the Prezi website, you can access the **Your Prezis** tab to edit, delete, or share a Prezi you have designed. If you are building Prezis for your business, there are some very important things to be aware of.

 If you are using the Prezi desktop application, you will need to upload your Prezi to www.prezi.com before you can share it with anyone.

Private Prezis

We obviously don't want to make our business presentations public so uploading a Prezi from the desktop application will automatically make them private. This means no one will be able to find your Prezi on the **Explore** tab by using the search box. Phew!

If for some reason you did want to make your Prezi public and searchable from the **Explore** tab, you can change the type of access with the following steps:

1. From the **Your Prezis** tab, click on the Prezi you'd like to share.

2. On the next screen click on the **Private** button in the upper-right corner just opposite your Prezi's title.

3. You can then change the access rights to **Public** or **Public & allow copy** as shown in the following screenshot.

 Only Prezi users with a paid license will be able to change privacy settings.

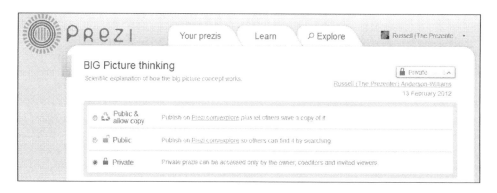

The three options shown in the preceding screenshot are as follows:

- **Public & allow copy**: Anyone can view your Prezi on the explore page of www.prezi.com and create a copy of it to modify themselves.

- **Public**: Anyone can view your Prezi on the explore page, but they won't be able to make a copy for themselves.

- **Private**: Your Prezi can only be accessed by the people you share its link with. These people can either view or edit the Prezi depending on the link you share with them.

Search engines

If you do decide to publish your company's Prezi to the **Explore** tab of www.prezi.com, then we're guessing it's because you do actually want people to find it and look through the information it presents regardless of who they are and what business they may be from themselves.

It's important to point out that the name and description you give your Prezis can be found by search engines. If you are really keen on people finding your design, then you might want to add your company name to these areas.

To change your Prezi's name and description, follow these steps:

1. From the **Your Prezis** tab, click on the Prezi you'd like to edit.

2. Hover over the title or description until you see an **Edit** link appear.

3. Click on **Edit** and type in a new title or description that contains your company name or relevant text for search engines to find.

Share this Prezi

Before we go into designing a Prezi for online use, it's important you know how to share your designs with colleagues, and the different ways in which this can be done.

When you click on the Prezi you want to share, you will see the **Share** button just below the Prezis preview window.

Clicking on this button will open up another screen that can be used to share your Prezi.

Viewing

Follow the given steps to quickly share your Prezi with colleagues.

1. Click on the **Copy** button on the right of the **Share** screen.
2. Paste this link into an e-mail and send it to anyone in your office that you'd like to view your Prezi.

Anyone who receives this link will be able to view your Prezi from `www.prezi.com`.

Editing

If you are working with someone on a Prezi design and would like them to make some changes, you can send them an edit link from the **Share** screen. Follow the given steps to do this.

1. Click on the **Editing** tab at the top of the **Share** screen.
2. Copy the link and paste this into an e-mail.

Whoever receives the link will be given full access to edit the Prezi online. This can be extremely useful when working across geographies.

At any time you can open the **Share** screen of your Prezi and click on the **Reset share links** button. This means that no one can now edit the Prezi unless they have the new link.

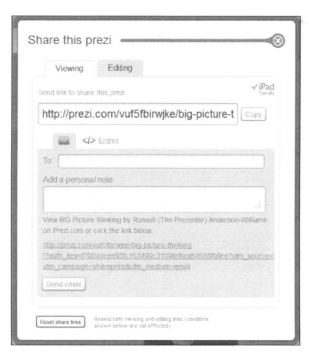

It's also worth knowing that by clicking the envelope button on the Share screen, you can send the links to view or edit your Prezi without the need to use Microsoft Outlook or another piece of e-mail software.

Embedding your Prezi

On the same share screen we've been looking at, you can also click on an **</> Embed** button that will enable you to embed your Prezi into a company website for all to see. This method of sharing a Prezi can give your design a lot more exposure when posted to company blogs, intranets, and your website. Depending on your level of knowledge and access to the areas above it can take a little longer to set up. Here we'll explain the fine details of how to embed your Prezi.

First of all, from the share page, click on the **</> Embed** link as shown in the following screenshot.

Prezi size

You can adjust the width and height of your Prezi by typing a value of pixels into the spaces provided. We would recommend you keep as close to the default measurements as possible, and definitely do not go any larger than width 800 pixels and height 600 pixels.

User experience

Once you are happy with your Prezis dimensions, you can then decide how your Prezi will work once embedded into a web page. The two options available to you on the embed screen are:

- **Let viewers pan & zoom freely**
- **Constrain to simple back and forward steps**

The option you chose will define the online user's experience. If you simply want to deliver a message, then keeping the Prezi constrained to back and forward steps will help. Letting users pan and zoom freely could make for a very interactive Prezi if designed correctly, but it could also mean your online users get lost in the canvas and quickly lose interest. Unless you design the Prezi really well, they might also miss important bits of content on your canvas.

 Later in this chapter, we'll look at how to approach a Prezi design that allows the user to explore on their own.

Embed code

That scary looking code on the embed screen is what you'll need to embed your Prezi into a web page. The code is written in **HyperText Markup Language** (HTML) which is the standard programming language of web pages.

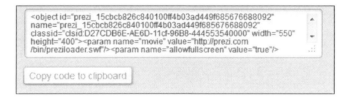

 You don't need to understand this code or be a programmer to embed your Prezi into a website, but if you have an in-house IT expert its worth being nice to them just for one day!

If you have access to your company's website and want to embed the Prezi into a web page follow the simple given steps:

1. Copy the code from the Prezi share screen.
2. Open the web page you want to insert your Prezi into.
3. Go into HTML mode and paste the code into the page.

4. Make sure to preview the page before you publish to the web. The following screenshot is a WordPress web page in HTML mode.

If you do decide to make changes to the dimensions of your Prezi, go back to the share screen and make adjustments there. As soon as you type in new dimensions, the HTML code will update itself as you can see in the following screenshot. Paste this new code into your web page.

It's also important to point out that when you embed a Prezi into a web page, you are simply creating a link between the website and your Prezi design on www. prezi.com. Should you change any content at all on your Prezi, it will automatically be visible through the web page with the embed code in it. You won't have to go through this entire process again once the Prezi is embedded.

You don't need to be a web guru to embed your Prezi, and this is a great way to share ideas and company messages with your colleagues.

 If your organization has a web developer that controls all the company's web pages, then make sure you're always nice to them. You never know how many times you might want to embed a Prezi and will need their help!

The online design approach

Designing a Prezi for online delivery needs a very different approach than designing for a face to face presentation. Because they will be viewing your Prezi online, and in their own time, you should assume their attention span will be very limited. Most people viewing content online only have about eight seconds before they become uninterested and move on to something else.

You should also assume that people might not know what Prezi is or how it works. This could send the technophobes in your office running straightaway.

In the rest of this chapter, we'll look at how to design your online Prezi with these things in mind.

The three Prezi design steps

The three design steps you learned about in *Chapter 4, Approaching Your Prezi Design* still apply:

1. Plan your Prezi.
2. Get the flavor right.
3. Build in layers.

In step 1, you need to make sure that you don't get too carried away with your ideas and stick to a very simple approach. No one is going to click through a Prezi that takes an hour to complete online, so try and make your content as simple as it can be. A no-frills approach is a good idea for online Prezis. You can still use step two to get a nice flavor and design.

Give instructions

Throughout your Prezi design you should always give the user instructions on how to navigate through the canvas. If people can't quickly grasp what they need to do then they might give up after only a few seconds. Tell the users exactly how to use it, and help guide them along the way.

A simple example of good instructions in the opening frame of a Prezi is shown in the following screenshot.

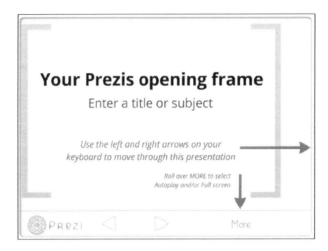

Even if the user hasn't used Prezi before, they should instantly know how to move through the Prezi above.

 Make sure your instructions are not too detailed, can be read in a few seconds, and stand out from other text that might be on the canvas. Use the arrow shapes from the bubble menu to point out certain areas to the user.

If your Prezi has been designed for the user to explore, then you will need to explain how they can move through the canvas. An example of this is shown in the following screenshot.

An even more powerful way of giving instruction while also engaging your audience would be to use a video in your very first frame. Using the knowledge you gained in *Chapter 3, Inserting a Video*, you can create a video that nicely introduces your subject, and also tells the user how to use the Prezi at the same time.

An example of this can be seen at `http://prezi.com/ir62lreumnyd/the-prezenter-prezume/` where a video is used after just a few clicks into the Prezi:

1. The Prezi is introduced and explained to the user.

2. The video finishes with instructions onscreen as well.

> **Click the right arrow to continue or just go and explore**

Adding instructions can really help improve the success of your Prezi. Remember that you don't have the advantage of being there with the person viewing it.

Embedded Prezis

If your Prezi is embedded into a web page, then add some simple instructions on the web page itself. Place them above or below the Prezi so that they are onscreen for the user at all times. An example of this can be seen in the following screenshot and is taken from `http://www.theprezenter.com`.

Narration

In *Chapter 2, Using Audio*, you learned how to insert audio into your Prezi. Mastering this skill can be extremely useful when designing for online use. The beauty is that your user will feel as though they are being presented to, and therefore, will be engaged from the start.

In your opening frame, add some narration introducing the subject and also explaining how the Prezi works.

Instructions

If you do use audio, make sure you have an instruction at the start that tells the user to turn up their speakers!

Highlighting

If you've designed a Prezi that's completely non-linear and that users can explore on their own then good for you. Make sure that your users don't get completely lost in the canvas though; otherwise, they will switch it off very quickly.

What you need to try and do is strike a balance between allowing them total freedom, and gently directing them to certain areas. You can do this by using simple markers to highlight where important information might be.

Highlighting with frames

The simplest way of doing this is using bracket frames to clearly highlight where a user can zoom in to view content. The following image shows a full Prezi canvas that a user could explore. Although the user can zoom anywhere they want to, you can clearly see where content is on the canvas.

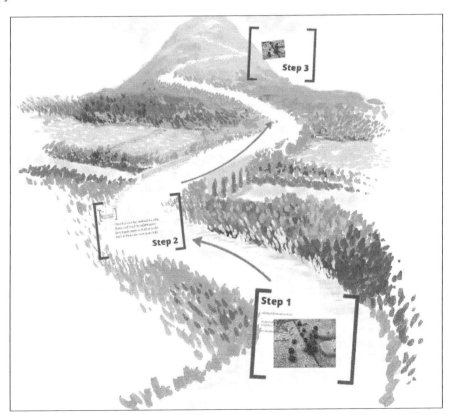

You can also add further details within frames as shown in the following image. There is no limit on how many levels of information you could add, but using bracket frames is a clear indicator that there is something here that needs to be viewed.

Add levels of content hidden within frames

Highlighting with color

If you're creating your own imagery, then you might want to be clever with your design and use color to highlight key areas. A good example of this can be seen at `http://prezi.com/jukqtsincrom/the-destruction-of-linea-learning`. In this Prezi, the users are encouraged to explore. Some clear instructions are given explaining how to do this, and the areas of important content are in a much brighter color than the rest of the imagery being used. There are no visible frames on the canvas at all.

The following screenshot shows clear instruction and good use of color to highlight key areas.

Invisible frames have been inserted around the highlighted areas to make it easier for the user to zoom in with just one click. You can see from the following example that it also has another level of content within the frame. If the user spots it and wants to zoom in, they can do so with just one click.

The following screenshot shows the same Prezi in edit mode.

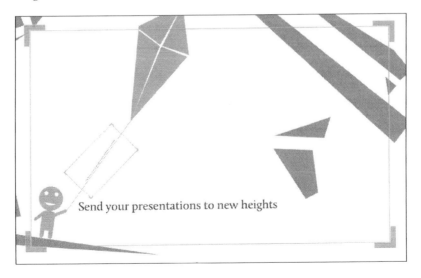

The good thing about using invisible frames is that they won't distract from any nice imagery you have. On the flip side of that it could mean that important information gets missed by the viewer. Using color, arrows, or even icons to highlight key areas is a must for any online Prezi design.

 Whichever technique you decide to use, always think about the user and try to strike the balance between giving them freedom and also guiding them to content areas.

Timing

How is your attention span when viewing content online? Like the rest of us, it's probably very low, and only a fraction of your "real world" attention span. If you use the techniques explained in this chapter so far, you'll be on track for creating a very engaging online presentation. What we don't want to do is ruin any initial engagement by creating a Prezi that takes 30 minutes to view from start to finish.

If your Prezi is non-linear and asks the user to explore on their own, then they'll probably complete it fairly quickly and leave it once they have the content they need.

If your Prezi follows a path, we strongly recommend that you try and design it to be no more than ten minutes long at the absolute maximum. And if you do build it to be delivered over ten minutes, we'd suggest you divulge the time it will take in your very first frame.

 Think about what your key message is and try and deliver it as quickly and as simply as you can. Do not try to deliver an hour long training session through an online Prezi.

The BIG Picture hook

In *Chapter 4, Approaching Your Prezi Design*, we explained to you how the BIG Picture technique works. If you use this technique very early in an online Prezi, it will grab the user's attention and engage them from the start.

Try to use the following structure when putting your online Prezi together with a path:

1. Give them an opening frame with instructions as explained earlier.

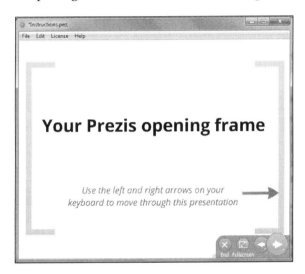

2. On the next transition zoom out to show them the whole canvas (the BIG Picture).

3. Now zoom back into the details and deliver the content.

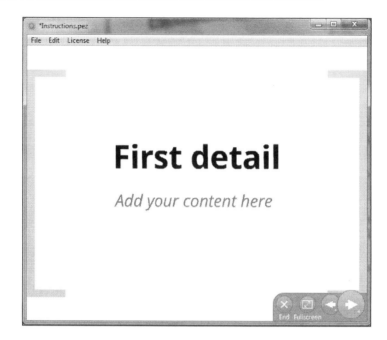

4. Zoom back out at the end to reveal the BIG Picture again.

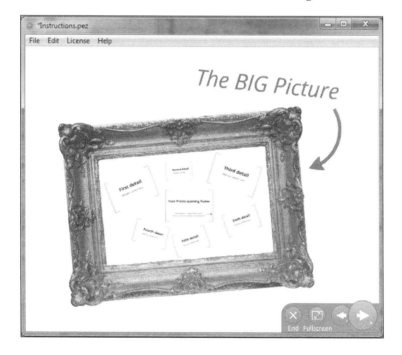

By doing this, you give the user an idea of the path they are about to follow. It will grab their attention and keep them engaged.

> **Imagery**
>
> Make sure you use some exciting imagery when revealing the whole canvas in step 2. The more visually stimulating you make your design, the more likely it will be viewed right to the end.

Summary

Being able to share your Prezis so easily is a brilliant feature of the software. However, if you do not take into account the simple points raised in this chapter your design is likely to fail. It probably won't engage your audience as you'd hope it would and this could mean you've wasted an awful lot of time designing it in the first place. Be realistic when you plan your online Prezi. People are extremely busy these days and normally have e-mail, web pages, Skype, and other distractions coming through their computer screens at them all day long.

If you want your Prezi's message to hit home and engage, then make it clear from the start what the user has to do, design your Prezi to look and sound great, and above all keep it short and to the point.

The next chapter looks at importing slides into your Prezi canvas. You might think it would be a sin for a Prezi master to even consider doing this, but in business it's a necessary evil that we have to face in most of our presentation designs.

7
Importing Slides into Prezi

In this chapter, we'll look at importing slides into your Prezi canvas. The Prezi master in you is probably shuddering at the thought of importing those nasty linear slides into your beautiful non-linear infinite canvas, but in business it can be a necessary evil. Knowing how to deal with it, and also how to deal with colleagues that don't use Prezi, are useful tools to have.

The chapter will cover the following:

- Why you'd import slides
- How to import slides
- Prezify your slides
- Things to look out for

Why oh why!

Every now and then a colleague may ask you if you could import some slides into a Prezi canvas for them. It may be because they have a very important sales pitch to a big client, they're presenting to the board, or they just want to look good when presenting this quarter's figures to their team.

If they have the slides already in PowerPoint or Keynote then why oh why don't they just use that? Do they really think that importing slides into Prezi is somehow going to magically make their presentation better than it was without any extra time or effort?

If anyone ever asks you to do this just smile and politely tell them you'll help, but then add the words **bear in mind that slides are still slides in any medium**. When they then ask what you mean you'll be glad you read this chapter.

Before we look at how to deal with this situation and Prezify slides let's understand exactly why we won't be able to escape this in business.

A bit of history

Another WHY you might have asked yourself since discovering Prezi is "Why does everyone rely on PowerPoint slides so much?" Well, don't blame them, it's not their fault that they think PowerPoint or Keynote are the only two presentation tools in the known universe.

Believe it or not, the concept of slide-based presentations has been around for about 300 years. To tell stories, people would paint onto glass and shine light through to project their images onto walls and engage their audience. Then, in 1955, a group of Americans developed the first ever 5 mm slide projector like the one in the following image. These used individual slides that the operator would have to physically remove and replace in order to change the image being projected.

For a couple of decades, we saw more powerful projectors come to market until one day those smart guys at Microsoft developed PowerPoint and gave everyone in business the opportunity to create their own slides and tell their own stories.

Since then, things have remained the same for nearly 30 years, and although we now have newer versions of PowerPoint with extra features and templates, people still don't realize that presentations don't have to be linear. They don't have to start at slide one and move through to slide 80 to tell their story.

The funny thing is that even when you introduce Prezi to your colleagues and explain the power of creating a non-linear presentation, chances are they'll nod appreciatively and then ask "Can I put my slides in it?" Again it's not their fault because all we've known for so long is linear slide-based presenting.

The next time you are asked to put a PowerPoint presentation into Prezi don't get mad. Follow the advice in this chapter and do your best to convert the colleague doing the asking over to the non-linear ways of the force!

Slides are here to stay!

As upsetting as it may sound to us Prezi masters, it is true. Slide-based presentations have been around for so long that businesses rely on them heavily to deliver important messages every day.

Because of this we have to accept that your business isn't going to ban the use of PowerPoint overnight and roll out your new Prezi initiative tomorrow. If it did, our words of advice would be to run away very fast. Trying to convert just one person over to non-linear thinking is difficult enough!

Slides are definitely here to stay, but as a Prezi master you have a great chance to convert colleagues over to Prezi and slowly introduce it into your business.

There's more advice on getting Prezi into your business in *Chapter 11, Getting Prezi through the Door.*

Slides are useful

As someone who will need to put together presentations for your business, you are going to need data and information. If your business is like most, then chances are that you'll find all the facts and figures you need on a PowerPoint file somewhere.

It's for this reason you should appreciate the fact that all your colleagues use PowerPoint or Keynote. If something appears on a slide, then it's entirely possible to bring that element into your Prezi canvas.

If you haven't already, then create a library of your colleagues' presentations and store them in one central location. That way you'll always have useful data for your Prezis

Another reason why

"CEO Bob saw a presentation done in that Prezi thing you like and he wants you to "jazz up" his slides for next week's product launch."

Sound familiar?

Another reason why you'll definitely have to work with slides is because Prezi's popularity is growing fast, but your bosses and colleagues having time to learn and appreciate Prezi is not going to happen as quickly!

We've heard lots of stories like this from Prezi users all over the world, so take some joy in knowing you aren't alone out there. A lot of business people just see Prezi as something a little more eye-catching than the usual presentation and don't understand the principles of non-linear formats or BIG Picture thinking.

You may be asked to "jazz up" some slides with Prezi from time to time, and using the tips in this chapter, you'll be able to do just that. As well as showing you how it's done, we've also highlighted some things to look out for along the way.

Importing slides into Prezi

A brand new feature available in Prezi is the ability to import PowerPoint slides from the **Insert** menu. To help explain how to use this feature, we'll use the PowerPoint slides shown in the following screenshot. They are very simple slides that have imagery, graphs, and, text.

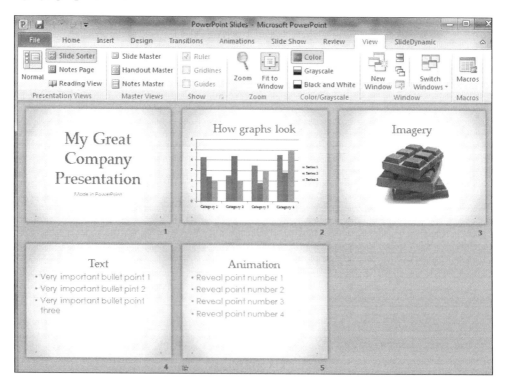

Once these slides are inserted onto our canvas, we will be able to manipulate all of the individual elements such as text, images, and graphs. This is something that Prezi users haven't been able to do for a long time, and is another great example of Prezi listening to the needs of its users.

The Insert PPT function

To import your PowerPoint slides into Prezi, follow the given steps:

1. Click **Insert** and then **PPT** from the bubble menu.

2. Select your PowerPoint slides to import and click **Open**.

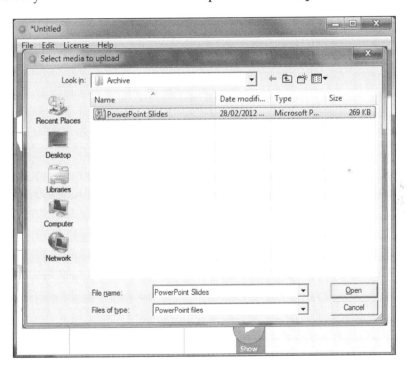

3. You will then see a sidebar appear on the right of your Prezi screen like the one in the following screenshot.

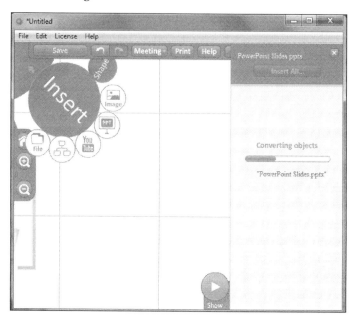

4. Once all of your slides are loaded into the right-hand panel, you can either drag individual slides onto the canvas or click **Insert All** at the top of the screen.

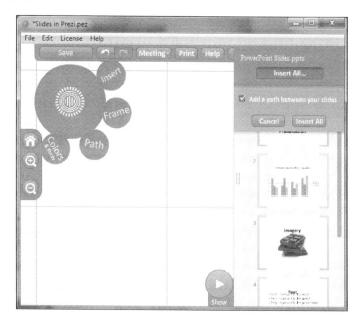

Tick the box "Add a path between your slides" to save yourself some time later.

5. Now position the slides' container in the correct position on the canvas.

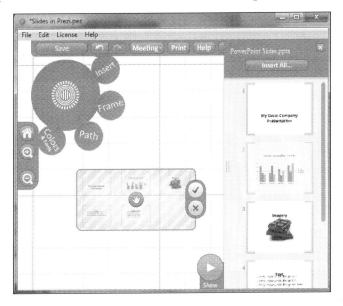

6. When you are happy with the slides' position, click the **green tick** to insert your slides.

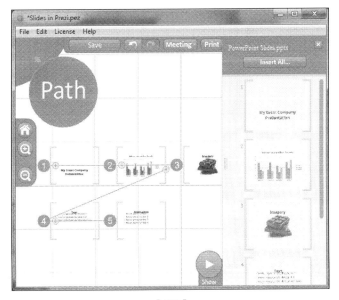

Please remember that it is possible to drag individual slides onto the canvas rather than using the **Insert All** function. In the following screenshot you can see we've dragged across slide 2 to our Prezi canvas. Clicking the **green tick** will finish the process and place slide 2 and all of its elements into our Prezi.

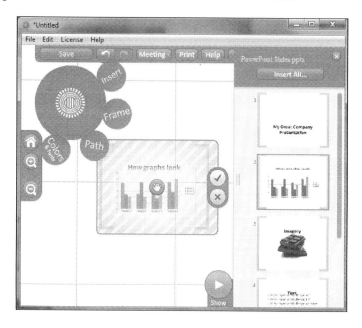

Prezify your slides

If you've followed the steps in the preceding screenshot, you can now start to Prezify your slides. This term simply means to add a new dimension to what are very linear (slide by slide) presentations. Here we'll look at a few simple tips to help bring your slides to life.

Positioning content

You can see from the following screenshot that on closer inspection of slide 2, the graph image is actually on top of the heading text. The title should read "How graphs look", but it's being overlapped and is unreadable to anyone viewing the Prezi.

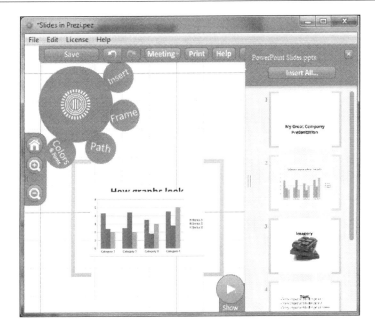

This will be the case for all of your slides, so the very first thing you should do is make sure all content is positioned correctly. Simple use of **Right Click** and **Bring Forward** or **Backwards** options will enable you to get everything as it should be.

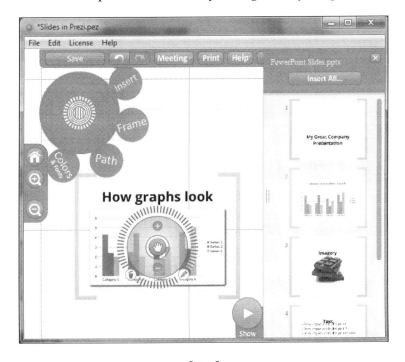

If you have a large number of slides, this task will take a long time to complete. If time is limited, you might want to skip to the last half of this chapter and look at the **Importing slides as .pdf** section.

Placement and frames

At this stage in becoming a Prezi master, we hope you're starting to think about your presentations more in the non-linear sense, and less in the straight lines of linear slide-based presentation techniques.

If that is the case, we'd like to think that the first thing you want to do when you see those slides appear on your canvas is to move them around and spread them out a bit.

This is the first real stage to Prezify your slides and helps give a more natural feel to the content rather than having everything in straight lines. The preceding screenshot shows a very simple example of how you might place slides onto your Prezi canvas, but the order and amount of space you use is entirely up to you.

 Remember you might want to zoom out and give an overview (BIG Picture view) to your audience, so place the slides well in order to show any relationships between them.

The Prezi **Insert PPT** function will automatically place a bracket frame around each slide for you. This is extremely useful for moving slides around, and of course, linking them to a path. If your presentation can logically be broken up into different sections, then we'd recommend you group the slides for each section together in another bracket frame as well. This will make it very easy for you or whoever is presenting to zoom out and give an overview, and then zoom into a particular section of interest.

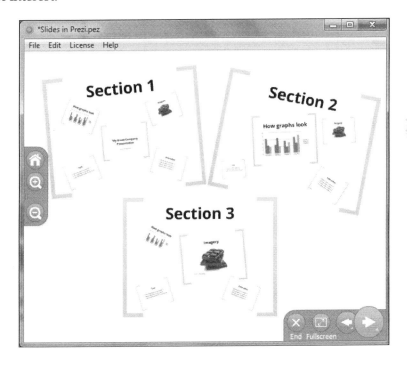

In the preceding screenshot, you can see that we've grouped several slides together and placed them in three separate sections. This will make it very easy for the presenter to zoom out and give an overview of the entire presentation. They'll also be able to zoom in on specific sections, and slides within those sections, very easily.

Zooming

Of course we'd recommend that you zoom into details as this will help give your slides an extra dimension. You might want to zoom in on imagery or text, but zooming can work particularly well with graphs that have been created in PowerPoint.

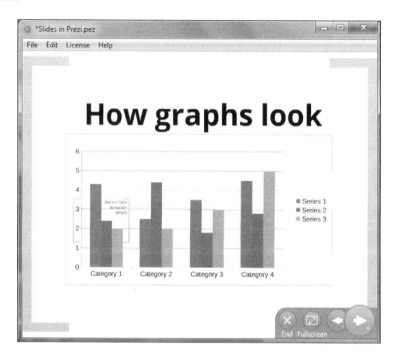

Graphs that have been created in PowerPoint will always be vector graphics. Because of this, when they eventually get inserted onto your Prezi canvas, they won't lose any image quality at all.

In the preceding screenshot, you can see how a graph looks on the Prezi canvas, and in the following screenshot, we've used a frame so that the presenter can zoom into a specific point on the graph.

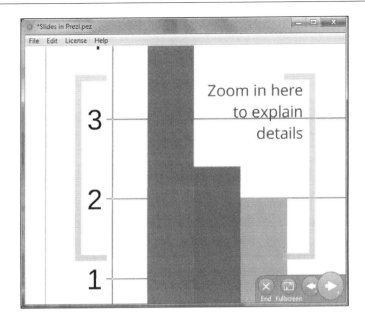

Graphs are great for displaying sales figures and other important management information, but they normally have too much detail and stay onscreen for 20-30 minutes while the presenter explains everything. Using the method explained here can really keep the audience engaged and give meaning to what is normally very dry content.

> If a graph has been imported into PowerPoint as an image, then it will be a raster image and not a vector (see *Chapter 1, Best Practices with Imagery*) once inserted into Prezi. Therefore, you will get some pixilation if zooming in too close.

No time to Prezify

Hopefully, you'll have time to use the **Insert PPT** function to the best of your abilities and turn those once-linear slides into something much more interesting. However, not all of us will have the time to reposition content for 50 or so slides, and spend the time required to fully Prezify our PowerPoint slides' content.

If time really is of the essence and you can't afford to waste a single second, you might want to try the following technique to insert your slides as PDF files. This will mean that once imported, everything will stay in exactly the same place that it was in PowerPoint, but on the flip side of that you won't be able to manipulate the individual elements of the slide.

Importing your slides as PDF

If you don't want to go to all the effort of re-arranging the content of your slides in Prezi and simply wish to import the slides as PDF images then follow these steps:

1. Open the PowerPoint or Keynote file you'd like to import.

2. In PowerPoint, go to **File** and click **Save As**, then save as a **PDF** file.

3. In Keynote, select **Share**, then **Export,** and click **PDF**.

4. Now open Prezi and select **Insert** and **Image**.

5. Select the **PDF** file you created in steps 2 or 3, and then click **Open**.

6. Your slides will then be placed in order on the Prezi canvas in order.

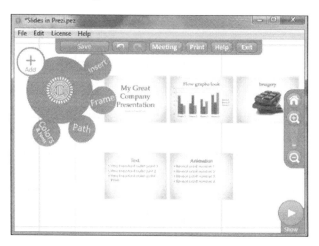

If you only want to insert a specific slide from your presentation, you will have to delete all other slides and then save or export the file as a PDF.

A classic mistake which we see made a lot is that once the slides are in Prezi, people simply link them together with a path and then brag to everyone that they've created a Prezi.

This is not the case at all, and as far as we're concerned, slides that have just been linked together on a Prezi canvas are still just slides and might as well of stayed in PowerPoint or Keynote.

 Remember to Prezify
Make sure that you use the steps explained earlier to Prezify your slides and utilize the space you have on the Prezi canvas.

Things to look out for

Inserting and prezifying your slides is great, but be careful and look out for the following items and don't let them catch you out and ruin your lovely Prezi.

Imagery

Because PowerPoint and Keynote don't have the functionality to zoom like Prezi does, they don't have to rely on such high resolution imagery. So long as the images on a slide look good enough when projected then that will normally work fine for the presentation.

Once these images are placed onto a Prezi canvas, you might decide that you want to zoom into them. If the quality isn't good enough, you could end up with the same pixilation problems we saw in *Chapter 1*, *Best Practices with Imagery*.

Zoom

If you are worried about the quality of images once they have been inserted into your Prezi, just use the zoom feature and check for pixilation. If you lose quality and you know things just don't look good, then delete the image and use Prezi's **Insert from web** function to find a new image of better quality.

Text

You are bound to have lots of important text on your slides. Before you import slides into Prezi though, there is one thing you'd really benefit from. Can you spot the problems with our following slide?

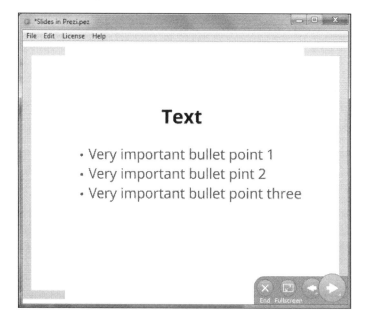

Hopefully, you've spotted that line two has a spelling mistake at the end (pint), and the end of the third line is formatted differently than the rest. These things are easily done, but they could also be easily missed once inserted into Prezi.

Spell check

Always run the spell checker in PowerPoint before exporting your slides to PDF format. It will save you lots of time and effort, and only take a minute to do.

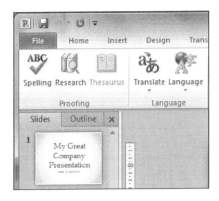

Animations

If you've used any slide-based presentation tool, you'll be familiar with animations. They are normally used to slowly reveal certain points as the presenter discusses them with his/her audience. They help engage a little more and used well enough, they can really help tell your story.

In the PowerPoint slide shown in the following screenshot, you can see that each bullet point is animated so that the presenter can slowly reveal them.

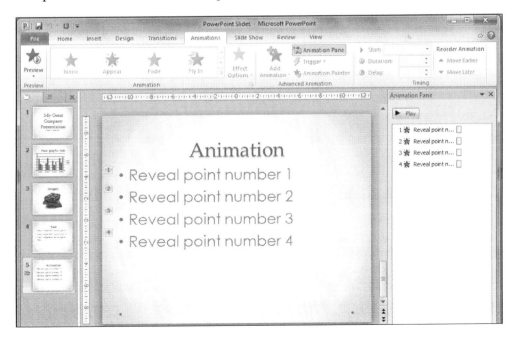

Prezi does not have any kind of animation feature like PowerPoint or Keynote. Any animation you've added in your slides will not transfer into Prezi. You can see in the following screenshot that once the same slide is inserted into Prezi all of the points are revealed at once.

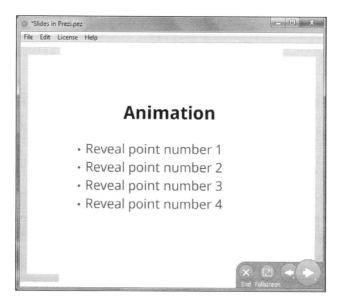

This may not be an issue for simple text animation as shown in the preceding screenshot, but if your animation is a complex one that involves imagery, you will need to address this before inserting into Prezi.

The solution

If your animation is a complex one, we'd suggest that you take it apart in PowerPoint. Lay the elements out on your slide in an order that makes sense. When you then bring the slide into Prezi, you can simply move from one part to the next and explain the connections.

Summary

By using all of the ideas we've mentioned previously, your presentation won't be recognizable from the PowerPoint or Keynote slides you started off with. As we mentioned at the start of the chapter, being able to Prezify slides is a necessary evil that every Prezi master should have in their toolkit.

Prezi's popularity is growing at a huge rate so if you're the company Prezi expert then expect to deal with slides a lot. While you're "jazzing up" your colleague's slides for them, try to explain why simply importing slides into Prezi doesn't make a good presentation. Make absolutely sure they know just how much time might be required to Prezify their slides, and maybe even send them a little checklist they can use before they send you anything:

- Check spelling
- Remove animations
- Supply high resolution imagery

That should be enough for them to come back and ask "Why do you need this done", at which point you can start to educate them. Trust us when we say, the more the number of people in your business that understand Prezi, the easier your life will be.

Good Luck.

In the next chapter, we'll look at using Prezi on tablets. In particular, we'll look at the Prezi iPad app and also explain how Prezi works on the Android platform.

8

Prezi for iPad and Android

Have you noticed more and more people in meetings with iPads or other tablet devices lately? Tablets are becoming extremely useful business tools for recording and sharing ideas. The market for these devices is becoming fiercely competitive, but there is still one clear winner (in terms of sales), the Apple iPad. A very close second are devices which run Google's Android platform.

This chapter will explain how Prezi can be used on either of these platforms, the benefits and downfalls of each, and also how you can make an impact by presenting a Prezi from a tablet device.

We'll cover the following topics:

- The Prezi iPad app
- Prezi for Android
- Choosing a platform
- When to use a tablet with Prezi

The Prezi iPad app

At the time of writing this chapter, the Prezi viewer app is at version 2.8 and it's fair to say that the app has come a long way since its first release in 2011.

Opening the Safari browser on your iPad, going to www.prezi.com and clicking into one of your Prezis will direct you to the App Store where you can download the Prezi viewer app. You won't be able to view your Prezis through the Safari browser on iPad because Apple devices do not support Flash content. This is one reason why a Prezi iPad app was needed in the first place.

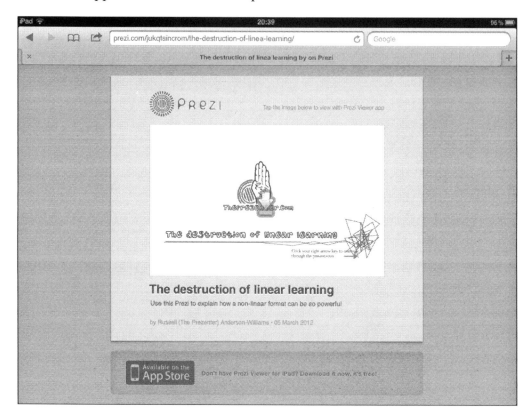

Using Prezi viewer

A quick search in the app Store for Prezi and you will find the Prezi viewer app which is free to download. Once installed, you can open the app and log into your Prezi account using the fields shown in the following screenshot:

Once your account details are entered, you will be taken into Prezi viewer where you can see all of your Prezis that are stored on www.prezi.com and also a selection of Prezis that have been specially selected by Prezi themselves as examples of great design.

 If you are using Prezi desktop on your PC or Mac and want to view your Prezis through the iPad app you must upload them to www.prezi.com first. Once uploaded to www.prezi.com, your Prezi will automatically be set to private, and so won't be visible to other Prezi users.

There are two main areas in the Prezi viewer app. The top area of the screen will show you any downloaded content you have while the bottom area will either display Prezis from your online account or the Prezi designs selected by Prezi.

You can switch between these views by pressing the **Your Prezis** or **Prezis we like** button on the right-hand side of the screen.

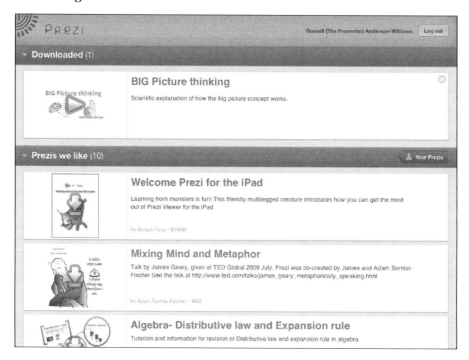

In the preceding screenshot, you can see that we have selected the BIG Picture thinking of Prezi used in *Chapter 4, Approaching Your Prezi Design* of this book, and added it to our **Downloaded** area.

To add a Prezi to your downloaded content, do the following:

1. Click on the **Your Prezis** button on the right to see a list of your Prezis from www.prezi.com.
2. Scroll through the list of Prezis and click on the one you want to download.
3. You'll then see it downloading and once it's ready, you'll be taken straight into that Prezi on your iPad:

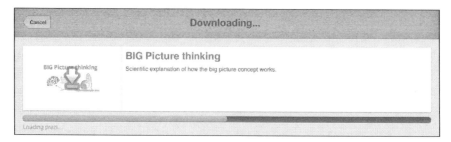

When you have a Prezi downloaded onto your iPad, you can view it offline. This makes it a brilliant business tool for sharing ideas with colleagues in meetings or just on the fly at coffee breaks and so on. It's definitely an impressive way to give your CEO an elevator pitch on your new business idea!

 If your Prezi uses YouTube clips you must have a wifi connection for them to work on your iPad.

Edit mode

When you open a Prezi in the viewer, you'll automatically enter Prezi viewer's edit mode:

1. In the following screenshot, you can see the hidden frames being used on the canvas, and in the center of the screen, there is an instruction to **Tap and hold any object to edit**.

2. Clicking on the **Question mark icon** in the top-left of the screen will give you a clue to some of the gestures you can use to edit your Prezi in the iPad viewer.

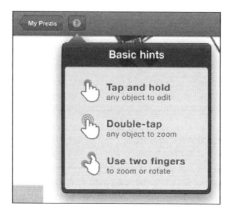

3. To move any object, simply **Tap and hold** it on the canvas.

4. As shown in the following screenshot, you'll then be given the option to **Edit** or **Delete**. If the object you're selecting is text, the iPad's keyboard will appear. If the object you've selected is an image, you will then need to use two fingers to either scale or rotate however you like.

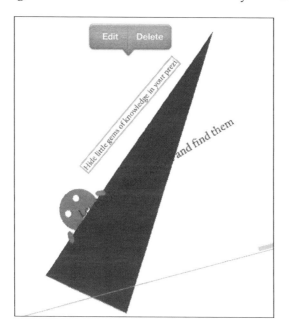

Editing your Prezi in the viewer takes a little time to getting used to. Like anything though, it'll soon become second nature to you if used enough. It's an incredibly powerful feature for making those last minute changes that you think of on the way to a meeting – especially if you spot an embarrassing spelling mistake just in time!

 Once you download a Prezi to the viewer on your iPad, you can make changes to it without the need for an Internet connection.

As this can be a little more difficult than using a mouse, those clever people at Prezi have put in a much needed the **Cancel** button in the top-left hand corner. This will only appear once you've made a change to the Prezi.

1. Once you have finished editing a Prezi and want to move back to the main menu, you can simply click on the **My Prezis** button in the top-left hand corner.

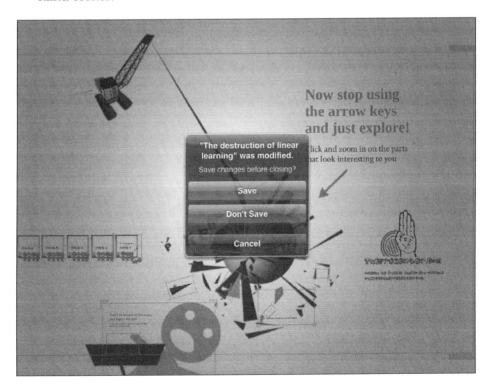

2. On doing so, you will then be asked if you'd like to save the changes you made.

 Any changes you make to a Prezi on your iPad will not link to the same Prezi in your account on www.prezi.com. We would suggest you only use edit mode in the Prezi viewer app for light retouches and editing text. Any major design work should be done in the original Prezi from your online account. Changes made there will feed through to your iPad so long as you have an Internet connection.

Show mode

Although you enter a Prezi in **Edit** mode there is a **Show** mode button located in the top-right of the screen at all times.

Clicking on this button will put the Prezi into full screen view so that all buttons disappear. To leave Show mode, there is a very subtle grey square in the top-right corner. Clicking on this will return you to edit mode.

Pressing the right or left sides of your iPad screen will move backwards and forwards through any path that you may have added. However, if your Prezi doesn't use a path (good for you) and is intended to be non-linear, you can move through it by using the touch gestures we all know and love on the iPad. This can really add a different dimension to your Prezi, especially if you are putting it in the hands of your boss or a colleague to explore.

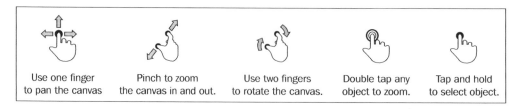

The preceding diagram shows you the different gestures available for use when viewing a Prezi. By now we are all familiar with these, but it's important to think about how they might have an effect on your Prezi design. For instance, do you need to add a frame if someone is going to pinch and zoom into your Prezi to look at more detail?

To get an overview of your Prezi and see the whole canvas, just give your iPad a shake.

Prezi viewer tips

There's no doubt that being able to present your Prezi on an iPad is a good thing. However, there are definitely some things we should make you aware of that will affect your design.

YouTube

When you download your Prezis to the Prezi viewer app, you will not be downloading any YouTube videos. These videos always stay on the YouTube website and your Prezi merely links to them and displays them.

This means that your iPad must have an Internet connection in order to view any YouTube content. Otherwise you will just end up with a blank screen and a message that reads "This content is not available offline".

It could be slightly embarrassing when you're trying to pitch a new idea to a colleague, or relying on a YouTube clip to deliver the punch line of your speech!

Sound

Prezi viewer for iPad will play sound files, but they will not behave or display as we saw in *Chapter 2, Using Audio*, of this book. In this chapter we looked at using sound and how to insert sounds into your Prezi. We showed you how to use imagery to cover up those ugly looking sound files so that everything looked (and sounded) perfect.

Unfortunately, all of the techniques explained in *Chapter 2, Using Audio*, will not apply when playing your Prezi through the viewer. These small glitches could change your design so we'd definitely recommend you try and test how sound works in the viewer first before spending hours on any design that uses sound heavily.

Images

In *Chapter 1, Best Practices with Imagery*, we explained the difference between vector and raster imagery. There were some obvious benefits for using vector imagery and inserting PDF or SWF files into your canvas. With these file types; you are able to zoom in on details without any loss of image quality at all.

Unfortunately, this is also not the case when using the Prezi viewer on iPad. The following screenshot was taken from the Prezi viewer and is of a Prezi file that only uses vector imagery.

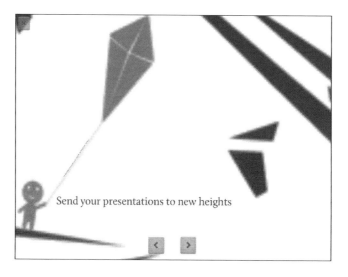

To see what the quality should be like you can view this Prezi at
`http://prezi.com/jukqtsincrom/the-destruction-of-linea-learning/`.

You can see that while the text (typed in Prezi) remains very sharp and clear, the imagery is extremely pixilated and does not look good at all. When viewing the same Prezi in a web browser on a PC, the imagery remains perfectly clear and there is no pixilation at all.

 If you are building a Prezi for use on an iPad, then you may want to avoid using vector graphics and stick to photos and images in raster format.

Prezi for Android

The Android platform and tablet devices that use it are rapidly starting to catch up to the Apple iPad in terms of popularity. Because of this, we thought it's only fair to give you an idea of how Prezi works on the Android platform as well, just in case you might be looking to use a tablet to present your Prezis soon.

Using Prezi with Android

The Android platform does have an extensive app market place, but there is no Prezi app available yet. "Well that's no good then is it?" we hear you shout. Don't panic, because if you have an android device running Android 3.2 operating system or below, Prezi works perfectly through Androids web browser which means you have full access to www.prezi.com and the **Your Prezis** tab.

 Unfortunately if you have a new android device that runs 4.1 Jelly Bean you wont be able to view any Prezis

Stay connected

As long as your Android tablet is connected to the Internet, you will have full access to the entire Prezi website. The downside is that if the connection is lost, then you cannot present any of your Prezis at all.

This may not be an issue at all within your organization if a wireless network is always available. If you do hit a wifi black spot though, it could be slightly embarrassing when your boss is waiting to see the presentation you've been so enthusiastic about. Make sure you know where those wifi black spots are and catch your boss at the right time and place.

Images

Using the Android browser to access your Prezis does not affect the quality of your images at all. In fact, they remain exactly as they would be if viewed through a laptop or PC.

The following diagram is a screenshot of the same Prezi we viewed in the iPad Prezi viewer app. It uses only vector graphics that are saved as PDF and SWF formats.

You can clearly see the images have remained crisp and clean just as intended in the design process. This is a massive benefit, and means you don't need to think about imagery when designing a Prezi to present on an Android tablet.

Editing

Because you are accessing your Prezis via a web browser rather than an app, you have full access to the online editor as well. This is a huge advantage as it enables you to make last minute changes to your design while on the move.

You can access everything from the Prezi bubble menu including frames, shapes, images, and, paths. The only limitation is that the text editor will not function properly. For some reason the keyboard does not appear when trying to add or edit text. Apart from this, every other object on your canvas can be enlarged or shrunk and rotated as you decide.

 Remember you will need to have an Internet connection in order to edit your Prezis via the Android browser.

Sound files

Inserting sound files in the same way as described in *Chapter 2, Using Audio*, will work perfectly via the Android browser. You may see a message appear onscreen saying "This video is not optimized for mobile" but the sound will still play as intended.

YouTube

Because you require an Internet connection to view Prezis on Android this means that your YouTube clips will play without any problems at all. They can be slightly temperamental at times depending on the strength of your Internet connection, but generally they play very well inside the Android browser.

iPad and Android comparison

As you can see there are benefits of using Prezi on either platform. The following table is a quick summary of both to help you decide which might be best for you before you go out and buy a new tablet device to show off to your colleagues.

	iPad	Android tablet
View Prezis when offline	Y	N
Retain image quality	N	Y
Play sound files	N	Y
Play YouTube files	Y	Y
Edit your Prezi offline	Y	N
Use prezi.com	N	Y

Obviously using Prezi won't be the only factor helping you decide which tablet to buy, but to a Prezi master it could be what clinches the deal.

When to present with a tablet

Being able to present your Prezi via a tablet opens up a whole new dimension for sharing ideas with your colleagues. Let's say that you have an amazing new business idea that you want to pitch to your boss. If you know that she/he prefers to see a visual presentation, but is too busy to sit down in a board room and wait while you fire up the projector, then using a tablet is perfect.

Open the Prezi on your tablet and put it into show mode, then simply put it in the hands of your boss and let them click through it while you stride along next to them on their way to their next important business lunch. If anything, they'll love the fact you're being innovative with how you present ideas to them. Make sure you get the tablet back though!

Don't assume your boss or colleague will know how to navigate the Prezi. Tell them how to click through it, but let them do all the work so that they are fully engaged in your presentation.

Brainstorming sessions are also a great place for you to use a tablet and run Prezi. You could place it in the center of a desk, or allow people to pass it around as they have an open discussion. You may want to show off (which we totally condone by the way) and connect your tablet to a projector.

 However and wherever you decide to present a Prezi with a tablet, make sure you let people hold it and play with it themselves. This makes for a much more engaging experience and one that hopefully they'll remember more of.

Projector + tablet = wow!

If you have an iPad 2 or new iPad you can link them to a projector using the Apple VGA Adapter cable which can be purchased from any Apple store. You can also do the same with Android tablets although there are so many different devices that run the Android platform that we'd advise you look into this before setting your heart on one particular product.

Using a tablet and projecting your Prezi can be a great experience for you and your audience, especially if you've designed your Prezi to be completely non-linear.

Firstly it will make navigating around your Prezi very easy for you because you're holding it in your hands. If someone in the audience wants to focus in on point C, you can simply touch that part of your Prezi to zoom in. Once done there you can give the Prezi a shake (a lovely feature) to return to the overview. If you are using a laptop you'd have to use a mouse and click on the screen. You'd either have to sit down or hunch over the laptop, so this makes for a much more natural experience.

If your room is set up well enough you might even be able to pass the tablet around to the audience and let individuals zoom in and share ideas they have on various points. By doing this, you're turning your audience into presenters and letting them know that their views are important.

This is a really exciting way to present and definitely makes for a much more interesting session. Don't be afraid to let your audience hold the tablet and zoom around. If you really are a Prezi master you might even want to hide snippets of information on the canvas for people to find as they do so.

Another benefit of using an iPad to present your Prezi is that you remove the need for a mouse to scroll and zoom around. This helps your Prezi look even better and means that your audience won't be distracted by seeing an arrow cursor on the screen.

A bit of fun

You may have seen some Prezis on the Explore page of www.prezi.com titled "Prezi + iPad =". These were all entries into a competition that Prezi held in 2011. To stand the chance of winning iPad 2, Prezi users had to create a Prezi explaining the benefits of the Prezi iPad app.

The winning entry can be seen at http://blog.prezi.com/2011/03/01/prezi-ipad-contest-we-have-a-winner/.

If you want to see a more comical Prezi which was one of the runners up, then go to http://prezi.com/yl9_u5si57pp/prezi-ipad-freedom.

There were hundreds of entries into this competition and they all give a great explanation of how beneficial the iPad app is.

Summary

Hopefully in this chapter, you've made some decisions about whether or not using tablets to present Prezis is going to work in your business, and if so which tablet you'd be best off using. Sure the iPad is a great device; it wouldn't sell millions and millions each year if it wasn't. Would the fact that Android devices don't have a Prezi app really stop you buying one? We don't think so but ultimately it's about you and how you work in your business that matters.

Whatever device you decide to buy (or already own), we really only wish for one thing. That you try and be as creative as you can with your Prezi design, and equally it's important that you give lots of consideration as to how you present it. Don't just let people see the screen without touching it themselves to have a play.

In the next chapter, we'll look at some of the new features released in Prezi over the last 12 months. How they work and more importantly how you can use them to make an impact.

9
Mastering the Newer Prezi Features

There's no question that Prezi is still very much in its infancy, and it's extremely exciting to think which features might be available in the coming years. Those clever Prezi boffins in the Prezi offices at Budapest and San Francisco are probably bubbling up some beautiful new features as you read this right now.

If you've used Prezi regularly for a while now, we're sure that it's changed quite a bit since you opened up your very first canvas, and maybe even since you opened up this book. The purpose of this chapter is to explore some of the new features available at the moment. Chances are that by the time you get to the end of this book, they'll be even more available to you.

We'll take a look at:

- Templates
- Shapes
- Drawings
- Text editor
- The plus button
- Grouping
- The play button

Templates

As we've talked about throughout this book, there will always be time restraints put on us when building any business presentation. Mostly these will be pretty unrealistic time restraints as well.

If you do find yourself against the clock when building a Prezi, then why not give yourself a slight advantage and use one of Prezi's templates to get your design started. There are lots of templates you can chose from and here's how to make the most out of them when the clock is ticking.

The templates

When you create any new Prezi online or in the desktop editor, you'll be presented with a choice of template as shown in the following screenshot

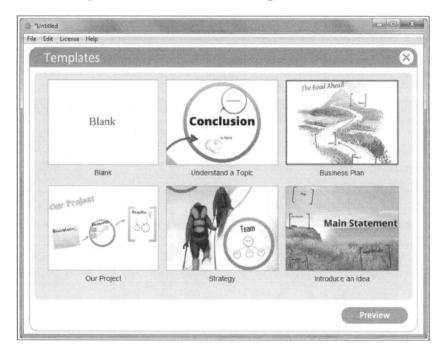

Before you decide which one to choose, you can explore them by simply selecting one and clicking the **Preview** button. You can see in the following screenshot that we've selected the **Our Project** template.

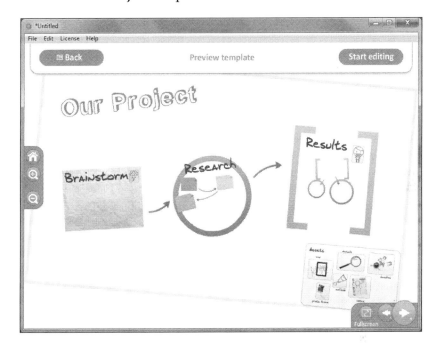

 Rolling your mouse over a template's thumbnail will show you some more details as well to help you choose.

At the top of the screen, you'll see the options to either **Start Editing** or go **Back** to the templates screen. Before you make your choice, have a look around the template preview and check out all of the various objects available to you. Zoom in and out of certain areas that look interesting and use the arrows in the bottom right to go through the template's path and see how it flows.

In the following screenshot, you can see that we've zoomed in to take a closer look at the assets included in this template.

As you can see in the preceding screenshot, the **OurProject** template has some lovely assets included. The assets you'll be able to use in the template are images and sketches such as the Doodles that you can see in the top right of the screenshot. All of these assets can be moved around and used anywhere on your canvas.

 Assets found in templates are explained in more detail later in this chapter.

If you preview a template and decide it's the right one for you to use, then just click the **Start Editing** button to go into edit mode and begin building your Prezi.

Getting the most from templates

Once you go into edit mode, don't think that you're stuck with how everything is laid out. You can (and should) move things around to fit with the message you're trying to deliver to your audience.

Paths

The very first thing we'd suggest is clicking on the **Paths** button and taking a look at how the Prezi flows. The whole reason you're using a template is because you're pushed for time, but you should know how many frames you need and how many different areas you'll want to focus on in your presentation before you get started. If you do, then you can adjust the paths, add new path points, or delete some that are there already.

Assets

All of the templates, especially **OurProject**, will come with various assets included. Use them wherever you can. It'll save you lots of time searching for your own imagery if you can just move the existing assets around.

As shown in the preceding screenshot, you are totally free to resize any asset in a template. Make the most of them and save yourself a whole heap of time.

Branding

The only down side of using templates is that they of course won't have any of your company colors, logo, or branding on them. This is easily fixed by using the **Colors & Fonts** | **Theme Wizard** found in the buuble menu.

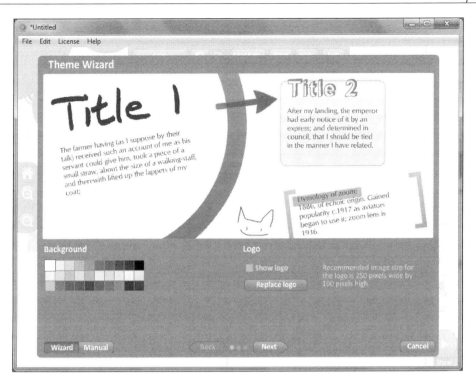

On the very first screen of the wizard, click the **Replace Logo** button to add your company logo. The logo must be a JPEG file no bigger than 250 pixels wide and 100 pixels high. Clicking the button will allow you to search for your logo and it will then be placed in the bottom left-hand corner of your Prezi at all times. On this screen, you can also change the background color of your entire canvas.

On the next screen of the wizard, we recommend you switch to **Manual** mode by clicking the option in the bottom-left corner. In this screen, you can select the fonts to use in your Prezi. At the present time, Prezi still has only a limited number of fonts but we're confident you can find something close to the one your company uses.

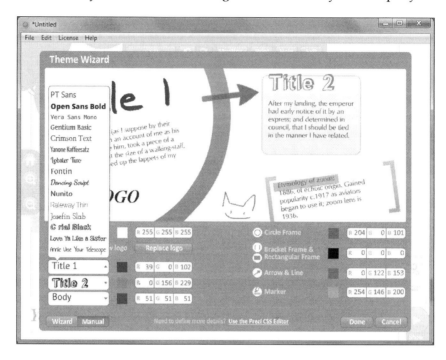

The reason we suggest switching to manual mode is because you'll be able to use your corporate colors for the fonts you select, and also on the frames and shapes within the Prezi.

 You'll need to know the RGB color values specified in your corporate branding.

By using this final step, you'll get all the benefits of having an already designed Prezi without getting told off by your marketing team for going against their strict branding guidelines.

Shapes

A very simple element of the Prezi bubble menu which gets overlooked a lot is the **Insert | Shapes** option. In this part of the chapter, we'll look at some things you may not have known about how shapes work within Prezi.

 Shortcut for shapes
To quickly enter the **Shapes** menu when working in the Prezi canvas, just press the *S* key on your keyboard.

Get creative

In the first part of this chapter, we looked at the assets from a template called **OurProject**. Some of those assets were the line drawings shown below the male and female characters.

When you see these "Doodles" as they're titled, you might think they've been drawn in some kind of graphics package and inserted into the Prezi canvas as you would anything else. On closer inspection in edit mode, you can see that each of the characters is actually made up of different lines from the **Shapes** menu.

This is a great use of the line tool and we'd encourage you to try and create your own simple drawings wherever you can. These can then be reused over time, and will in turn save you lots of time searching for imagery via the Google image insert.

Let's say that we want to add some more detail to the male character. Maybe we'll give him a more exciting hair style to replace the boring one that he has at the moment.

1. First select the current hairline and delete it from the character's head.

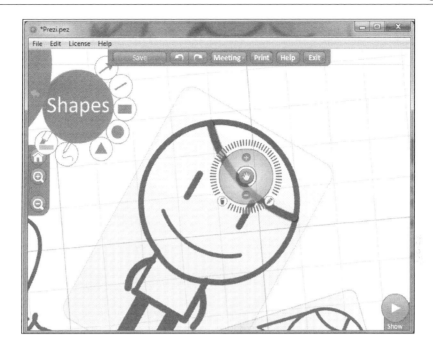

2. Now select the line tool from the **Shapes** menu and let's give this guy a flat top straight from the 80's.

3. One of our lines is too long on the right. To adjust it, simply double-click to enter edit mode and drag the points to the right position as shown in the following screenshot.

So there we have a great example of how to quickly draw your own image on the Prezi canvas by just using lines. It's an excellent feature of Prezi and as you can see, it's given our character a stunning new look.

It's a shame his girlfriend doesn't think so too!

Editing shapes

In step three of giving our character a new haircut, you saw the edit menu which is accessed by a simple double-click. You can use the edit function on all items in the shapes menu apart from the Pencil and Highlighter tools. Any shape can be double-clicked to change its size and color as shown in the following screenshot.

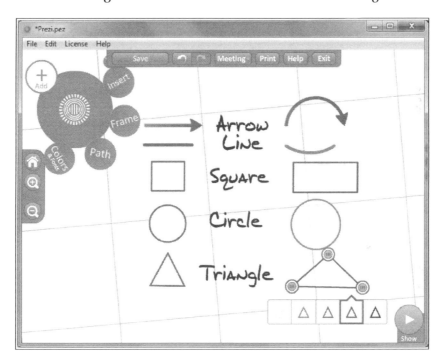

You can see that all of the shapes on the left have been copied and then edited to change their color and size. The edited versions on the right have all been double-clicked and one of the five extra available colors have been selected. The points of each shape have also been clicked on and dragged to change the dimensions of the shape.

[Holding the *Shift* key will not keep your shapes to scale. If you want to scale the shapes up or down, we recommend you use the transformation zebra by clicking the plus (+) or minus (-) signs.]

Editing lines

When editing lines or arrows, you can change them from being straight to curved by dragging the center point in any direction.

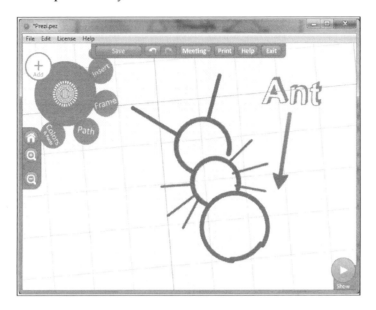

This is extremely useful when creating the line drawings we saw earlier. It's also useful to get arrows pointing at various objects on your canvas.

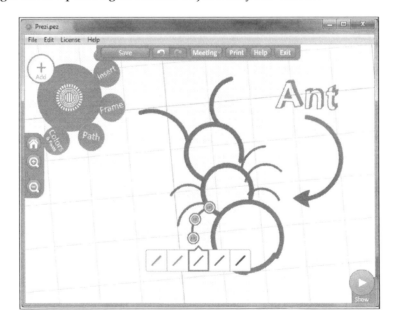

Highlighter

The highlighter tool from the shapes menu is extremely useful for pointing out key pieces of information like in the interesting fact shown in the following screenshot.

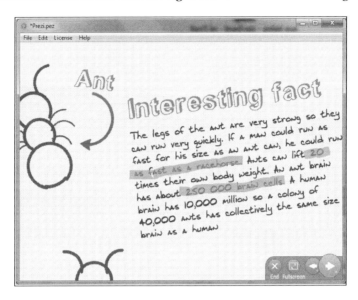

Just drag it across the text you'd like to highlight. Once you've done that the highlighter marks become objects in their own right, so you can use the transformation zebra to change their size or position as shown in the following screenshot.

Pencil

The pencil tool can be used to draw freehand sketches like the one shown in the following screenshot. If you hadn't guessed it yet, our drawing is supposed to represent a brain which links to the interesting fact about ants.

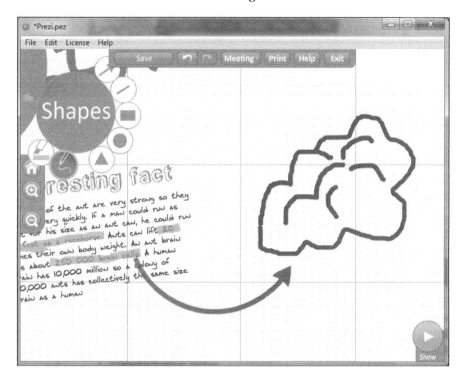

The pencil tool is great if you're good at sketching things out with your mouse. But if like us, your art skills need a little more work, you might want to stick to using the lines and shapes to create imagery!

 To change the color of your highlighter or pencil drawings, you will need to go into the Theme Wizard and edit the RGB values. This will help you keep things within your corporate branding guidelines again.

Drawings and diagrams

Another useful new feature and a big time saver within the Prezi insert menu are drawings and diagrams. You can locate the drawings and diagrams templates by clicking the button in-between YouTube and File from the **Insert** menu.

There are twelve templates to choose from and each has been given a name that best describes their purpose. Rolling over each thumbnail will show you a little more detail to help you choose the right one. Once you have chosen, double-click the thumbnail and then decide where to place your drawing on the canvas. You can see in the following screenshot that the drawing or diagram is grouped together and will not become active until you click the green tick.

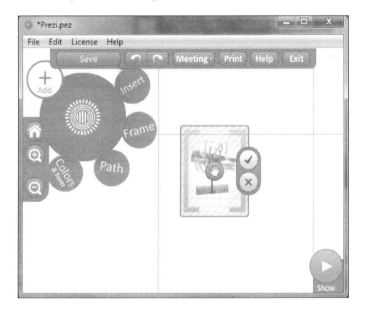

Once you make the drawing active, you can access all of its frames, text, and any other elements that are included. In the following screenshot, you can see that we've zoomed into a section of the tree diagram.

You can see in the preceding screenshot that the diagram uses lines, circular frames, and text which can all be edited in any way you like. This is the case for all of the diagrams and drawings available from the menu.

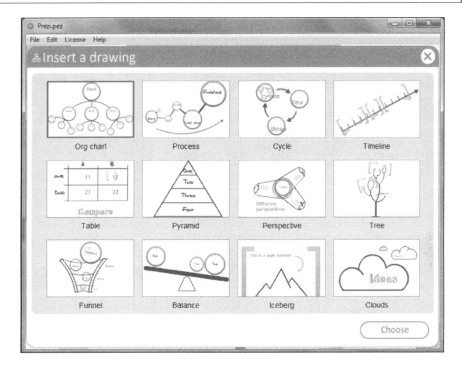

Using these diagrams and drawings gives you a great chance to explain concepts and ideas to your colleagues with ease. You can see from the preceding screenshot that there's a good range of useful drawings and diagrams that you're used to seeing in business presentations. You can easily create organograms, timelines for projects, or business processes and cycles, simply by using the templates available and inserting your own content and imagery.

 By using the Theme wizard explained earlier in this chapter, you can make sure your drawings and diagrams use your corporate colors.

Prezi text editor

The text editor in Prezi has had a wonderful makeover in recent months. There are now some lovely new features within it that will make your life much easier, including the number one must have feature at the very top of every Prezi user's wish list for some time. Yes you guessed it, a spellchecker!

Spellchecker

Now when you spell something incorrectly, Prezi will underline the word it doesn't recognise with a red line. This is just as you would see it in Microsoft Word or any other text editor.

To correct the word, simply right-click it and select the word you meant to type as shown in the following screenshot.

It's been a long time coming, but it's finally here.

Text drag-apart

So a colleague of yours has just emailed you the text they'd like to appear in the Prezi you're designing for them. That's great news as it'll help you understand the flow of the presentation. What's frustrating though is you'll have to copy (*Cti+ C*) and paste (*Ctr+ V*) every single line or paragraph across to put it in the right place on your canvas.

Or at least that used to be the case before Prezi introduced the drag-apart feature in the text editor. This means you can now easily drag a selection of text to anywhere on your canvas without having to rely on the copy and paste options. Let's take a look at the interesting fact info we saw earlier and split it up into two sections.

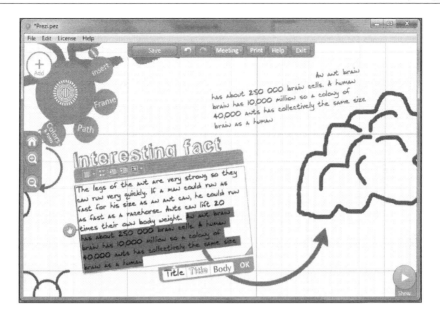

In order to drag your text apart, simply highlight the area you require, click the hand icon to the left and hold the mouse button down, then drag the text anywhere on your canvas.

Once you have separated your text, you can then edit the separate parts as you would any other individual object on your canvas. Use the transformation zebra to scale it or spin it around as shown in the following screenshot.

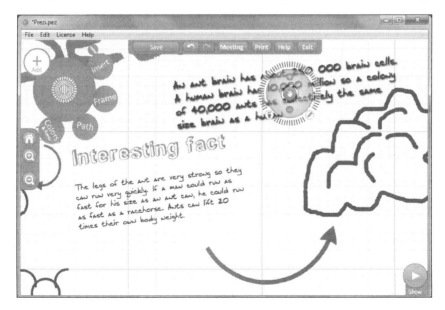

Building Prezis for colleagues

If you've kindly offered to build a Prezi for one of your colleagues, ask them to supply the text for it in Word format. You'll be able to run a spellcheck on it from there before you copy and paste it into Prezi. Any bad spellings you miss will also get highlighted on your Prezi canvas but it's good to use both options as a safety net.

Font colors

As well as dragging text apart to make it stand out more on its own you might want to highlight certain words so that they jump out at your audience even more.

The great news is you can now highlight individual lines of text or single words and change their color. To do so, just highlight a word by clicking and dragging your mouse across it. Then click the color picker at the top of the textbox to see the color menu shown in the following screenshot.

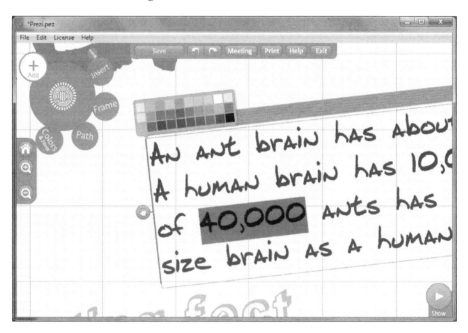

Select any of the colors available in the palette to change that piece of text. Nothing else in the textbox will be affected apart from the text you have selected. This gives you much greater freedom to use colored text in your Prezi design, and doesn't leave you restricted like in older versions of the software.

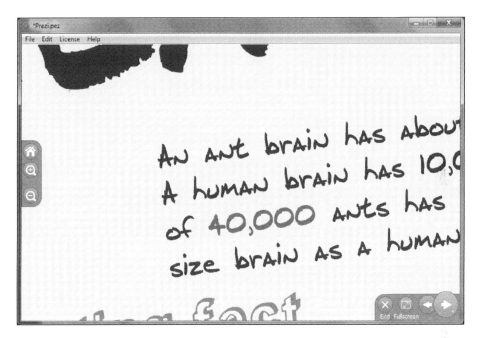

Choose the right color

To make good use of this feature, we'd recommend you use a color that completely contrasts to the rest of your design. For example, if your design and corporate colors are blue, we'd suggest you use red or purple to highlight key words. Also once you pick a color, stick to it throughout the presentation so that your audience knows when they see a key piece of info.

Bullet points and indents

The final new feature within the text editor is the option to use bullet points and indentations. This makes your business presentations much easier to put together and does mean you can give the audience some quick fire information as text in the same format they're used to seeing in other presentations.

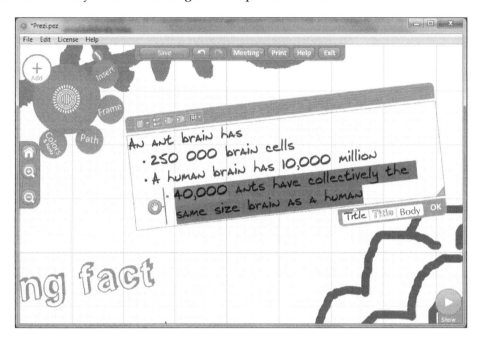

In the preceding screenshot, you can see we've taken the same text that we dragged apart earlier and added bullet points to it. This was done by simply selecting the main body of text and clicking on the bullet point icon at the top of the textbox. To add indentations to your bullet points, use the icons to the left of the color picker.

A really simple features but a useful one none the less. We'd obviously like to point out that too much text on any presentation is a bad thing. Keep it short and to the point.

 Also remember that too many bullets can kill!

The plus (+) button

Throughout this book and certainly in this chapter, we've helped make you aware of the time-saving elements that Prezi features can bring to your busy business day. The plus button located on the left of the bubble menu is an incredible time saver, and also helps keep your Prezi's style looking consistent throughout.

Clicking the plus button will open up a selection of five different layouts for you to choose from. You can see these in the following screenshot.

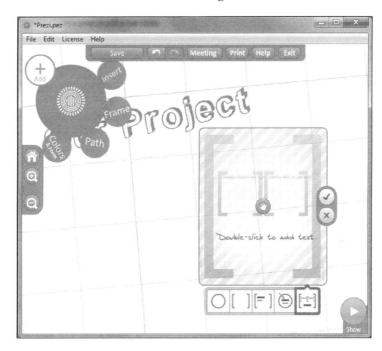

Some are simple empty frames but others have textboxes in them ready to use straightaway. When you're happy with the layout you've selected, click on the **green tick** to insert it onto your canvas. You can now type or paste in any text that's needed in your presentation, or add imagery into the layout.

[**Shortcut**
Press the *N* key on your keyboard to access the plus button.]

Scaling layouts

An amazing feature within the plus button is that the layouts will automatically scale to the objects you place them next to on your canvss. In the following screenshot, you can see there is already a frame and layout on our canvas. Before we select the new layout from the plus button, we can drag it towards the existing frame and see it start to shrink in order to match the size of the frame we're placing it next to.

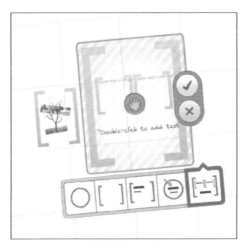

In the following screenshot, you can see that as we drag the new layout towards the existing frame, it starts to shrink in order to match the size.

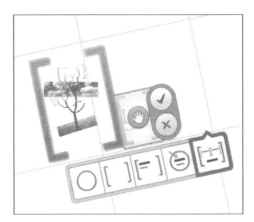

This is an extremely useful feature that helps us place things at the right location and in the right size without wasting any time trying to adjust it ourselves. Give it a go so you know exactly what we mean.

Consistency

Just like we mentioned earlier with the Theme wizard, it's crucial you try and keep a consistent style running through your presentation. This includes your colors, fonts, highlights, and of course the way in which you lay out your frames and text. Try and stick to the same layout from the plus button throughout your Prezi.

Grouping and moving

In the past, it was difficult to move lots of separate elements at once. You'd have to try and select them all at once and then move them. Now you can choose one of the two options to easily move lots of objects around on your canvas. We'll use the ants we saw earlier in this chapter because they are made up of lots of separate curved lines placed together. How on earth could we move all of those lines at once?

Using a frame

One way to move all of the ant's separate parts is to drag a frame around it. Once the frame surrounds all of the objects you want to move, you can select it and drag it anywhere as you can see in the following screenshot.

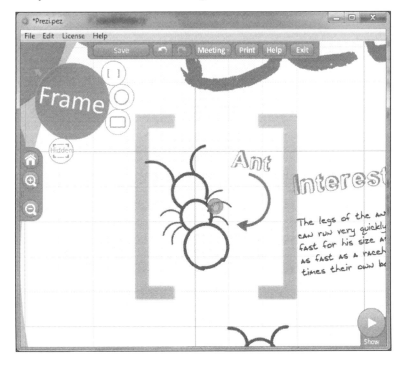

Once you've moved the objects to a new spot on your canvas, you can delete the frame.

 Hidden frames are the only frame type that this won't work with.

The Shift key

Another way, and probably a slightly easier way of moving lots of objects at once is to simply hold the *Shift* key down on your keyboard and drag across the canvas to select all the objects you need.

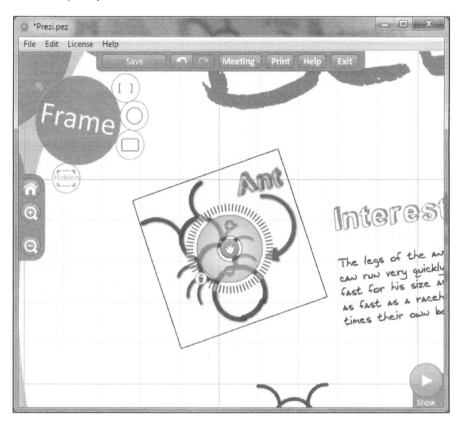

This is probably a function that mostly will be used to in other bits of software so its bound to be a preferred option here.

Whichever option you use to move objects around, you're bound to save lots of time doing so. Either of the preceding options will allow you to move, enlarge, shrink, or rotate a group of objects. This used to be something that would put people off using Prezi, but now it's just a normal run of the mill feature. Hallelujah!

The play button

The play button is located down in the bottom-right hand corner and is what we use to put our Prezis into show mode to check that they look okay during the design phase. It is then later used used of course when our Prezis are actually being presented. There is a lovely new feature that most forget about or just don't notice that could help you when designing a Prezi to play on its own.

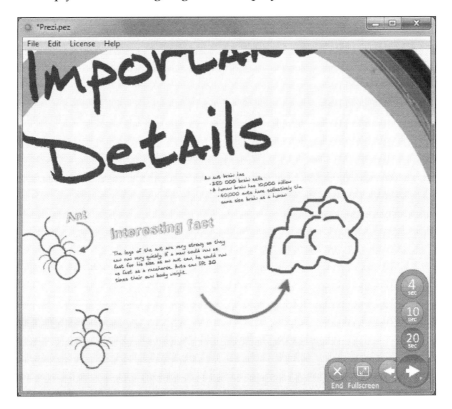

You can see in the preceding screenshot that the bottom-right arrow key is displaying three separate time settings:

- 4 seconds
- 10 seconds
- 20 seconds

To access these, simply click and hold the right arrow key with your mouse. When they appear, you can select the timing you'd like your Prezi to play at.

This is useful for presentations that don't have a presenter to talk through them. They might be showed in your company's reception on a flat screen, or at a trade show for people to see. However and whenever you decide to let your Prezi play on its own, make sure you get the timings right so that people can see and read everything without having to wait until it loops again.

 When designing Prezis to play on their own in this way, make sure you pay close attention to the amount of zooming and spinning in your design. Motion sickness can be intensified when someone is overly focused on the screen in front of them.

Summary

We're extremely confident that by the time you've read this chapter, there will be even newer features available to you in Prezi. One great thing about being a Prezi user is, there is lots to look forward to in the future. Just make sure you put every new feature to good use, and make it work for you to save as much time as possible.

In the next chapter, we'll be looking at Prezi meeting and will show you how to use it for group brainstorming or presenting to overseas colleagues or clients.

10
Prezi Meeting

Want to save your colleague's hours of travel time? Want to be able to tell your boss you've lowered spending on fuel for company vehicles by 50 percent? Would you also like all your colleagues to think "Wow that guy is a genius"? Then you'll definitely want to pay full attention to this chapter because Prezi can help you and your business save huge amounts of valuable time, while making you look pretty awesome at the same time.

For some time now, Prezi has offered its users the ability to collaborate in online presentations. While more and more pressure is being put on business people all over the world, the less time we all have to travel huge distances. It simply doesn't make sense anymore for you or a colleague (or both) to travel half way across the country for an hour's presentation or brainstorming session. Why not do it all online via Prezi meeting, cut down the emissions, and be home in time for your kid's soccer game?

Prezi meeting allows you to invite guests and/or collaborators onto your canvas. You can either invite them to just view your presentation, or they can receive an invite to edit the canvas with you. All of this is done via `www.prezi.com` and is incredibly easy to set up.

In this chapter we're going to look at:

- How to invite online collaborators
- Editing a canvas together
- Presenting online
- Controlling the session
- Removing access

Setting up a Prezi meeting

The very first thing to mention is that Prezi meeting can only be used online via www.prezi.com and not from the Prezi desktop application. If your Prezi is already online, then just click on the **Edit Prezi** button and skip this section of the chapter. If you have built a Prezi in the desktop application and want to present it online, you'll need to upload it first. Follow these steps from the Prezi desktop:

1. Click on **Prezi Meeting** at the top of the desktop application.

2. Select **Start online Presentation** if you are simply presenting:

3. Give your Prezi a **Title** and **Description** in the fields that appear, and then click on **Start Upload**:

4. Once the upload to www.prezi.com is complete, click on the link provided to go straight to the online version of your Prezi:

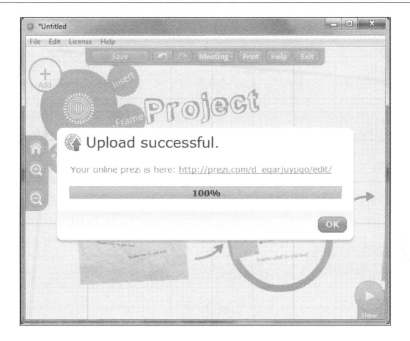

The preceding steps will take you directly into the online version of your Prezi. You can also go to **File | Upload to prezi.com** to upload from the desktop application. If you do this, you'll still have to enter a Title and Description, but you'll then need to go to www prezi.com and open the Prezi yourself.

Once you have performed all of the preceding steps, you can close the Prezi desktop. For the rest of this chapter, we'll work from your new online canvas. Next, we'll see how to send invitations out, and then some more details on actually running an online session and getting the most from Prezi meeting.

Sending invites

Now that we are in our online canvas, we can send out invites to anyone whom we want to join us. Here we'll take a look at how it's done, and the details behind presenting online or allowing others to edit.

[There is currently a limit of ten users allowed in a Prezi
meeting at one time.]

Invite to an online presentation

In your online canvas, go to the **Meeting** menu at the top of the screen and select **Start online presentation**:

When the preceding box appears, you will need to copy the link and e-mail it to anyone you wish to join. Once they click on the link, they will automatically be taken into your canvas as a guest and you will see them appear as a small avatar at the bottom of the canvas. You can see this in the following screenshot:

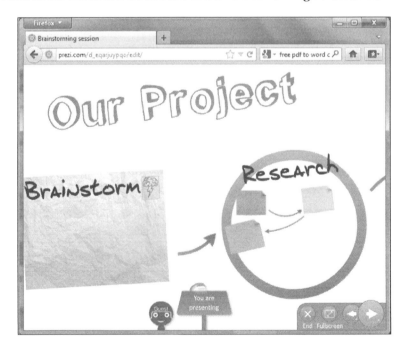

We'll go into more detail on how these funny little characters can be controlled by you and the guest later in the chapter.

Invite to edit

In your online canvas, go to the **Meeting** menu at the top of the screen and select **Invite to edit**. You will then see the same kind of screen as we did previously, except that this link will allow people to edit your canvas:

The warning message at the bottom of the screen is to make you aware that people can start editing your Prezi immediately. They will also be able to do this for one week until the link expires.

 Make sure you send out these invites a few minutes before you start the session. Any time it is sent earlier, people might be tempted to log in and play/break your presentation!

Copy the previously given link into an e-mail and send it to anyone you wish to attend and edit your Prezi. Because you are allowing them to edit, they must register as a Prezi user to access the session. This is something worth mentioning in your invite e-mail. Remind them that it's free; they only need to enter an e-mail address and password, and it's a great tool for online meetings in the future.

Just as it did in the previous section for invites to your online presentation, your guest's avatar will appear at the bottom, of the screen. This time you will be able to see their name written across the avatars head:

The invitation e-mail

Remember that using Prezi is probably going to be very new to the people you're inviting. Because of this, you need to make sure you don't confuse them from the very start. Keep the invitation e-mail brief, and if you are going to be using a telephone conference line to talk to one another, then make sure it's mentioned in the e-mail as well.

Presenting online

The simplest option to use and manage in Prezi meeting is an online presentation. This literally allows you to take a group of invited guests through a presentation that you've designed. If you have a path in your Prezi, then moving to each stage will also move the guests along with you as well. If your Prezi doesn't have paths, you can zoom around freely and your guests will also move along with you.

Audio

We obviously recommend you use some kind of audio system to speak with your guests as well. Prezi doesn't have any built-in function for using audio, so a company conference line or Skype will be sufficient enough. Make sure you mention the audio details on your invite, and also in the very first frame of your Prezi link we have in the following screenshot:

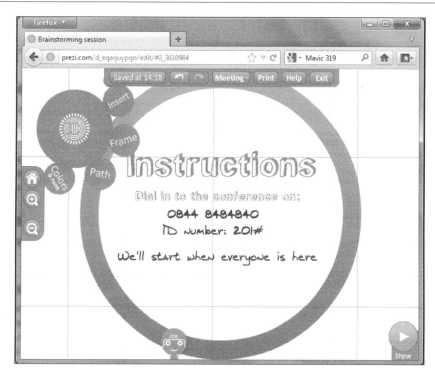

Where have they gone?

The only real danger you face when presenting online through Prezi meeting is losing people on your canvas. Because Prezi might be so new to people, they'll get excited and probably click on anything they can. If they click on your avatar at the bottom of the screen, they may stumble upon the following message:

When they click **explore freely**, they'll be released from following you and can roam around anywhere they like. This could be okay as they might be exploring more details of your Prezi but if you want them to follow you just make sure you ask them not to click that option until the end of your presentation. The promise of being allowed some freedom might be enough to keep them behaving for now!

Timings

We gave the same advice earlier in this book, but it's worth repeating here. If you are presenting online, remember your audience's attention span will be limited. Keep the presentation as short as possible, and make it as visually engaging as you can with imagery and video.

Editing online

Allowing people to edit your Prezi can be a scary thought, but in this section we'll look at how best to approach it. We'll also give you some useful tips to help keep people focused.

This can be an extremely powerful way of brainstorming new ideas with colleagues in other locations. Even if you just have to walk a few flights of stairs to get to them, you might want to try this and save those legs of yours!

Following are some useful things to think about when running an online collaboration or brainstorm.

Instructions

Make sure that the very first thing they see on your canvas is a set of instructions like the ones we saw on the previous page with audio instructions on.

Entering the session

You might find that when your guests arrive onto the canvas, they do so in show mode. Once everyone has arrived, ask them to press the **End** (x) button on the bottom right so that they can edit the Prezi.

Practice area

Having a practice area that people can play in will help them get familiar with the software before you start the session. In the practice area shown in the following screenshot, you can see that we've asked our guests to zoom into a certain area.

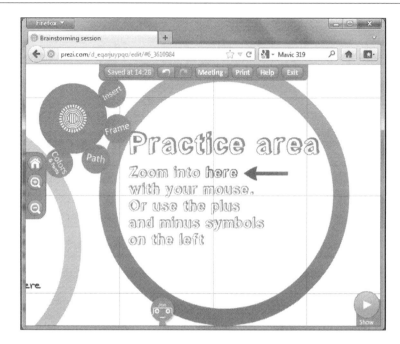

Give your group the instruction and then zoom in there yourself and wait for people to arrive. You'll know if they are there yet because their avatar will turn into a circle and arrow indicating their location.

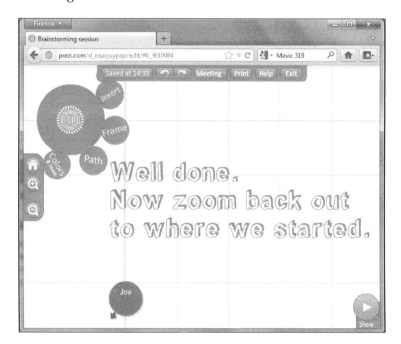

You can see in the preceding screenshot that Joe isn't yet in the right spot that we've told him to go to. When you see the full avatar of each person on your canvas, you can be sure that they are now at the same spot as you.

You might also want to add some practice exercises on:

- Adding text
- Inserting images
- Frames
- Shapes

> We'd advice you to tell people not to use the Paths feature. This could get messy, especially if people are working in different areas of the Prezi.

Chat area

Because there isn't a chat box like you'd see in a virtual classroom, why not set up a dedicated area for people to chat in? Tell them they can go there any time they like to post questions which will later be addressed, or instruct them to go there when your brainstorming session comes to a logical break. This just adds a bit of fun to the session, and could give you a good insight into what people are thinking about the session.

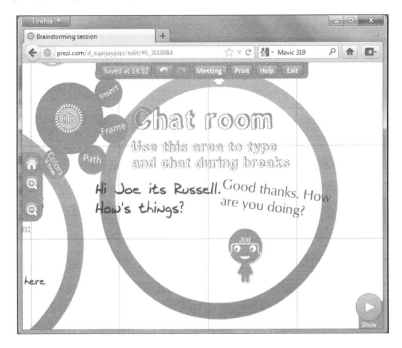

Personal space

One way of running a great brainstorming session is to first give people the instructions and practice, and then let them work in their own personal space for a while.

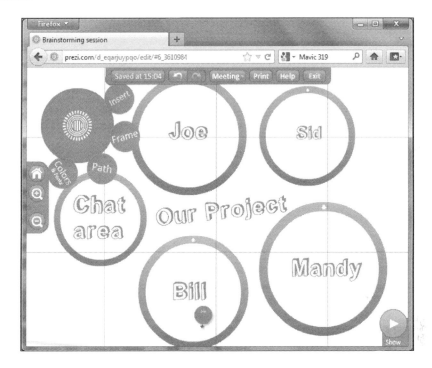

Give them a specified frame with their name in and set them the task of generating as many ideas as they can in a certain time limit. Once they've all done some brainstorming, you can move around as a group and let each guest talk through their ideas.

You could even create a separate frame titled "Best bits" and copy paste all the best ideas to it for everyone to see in one place.

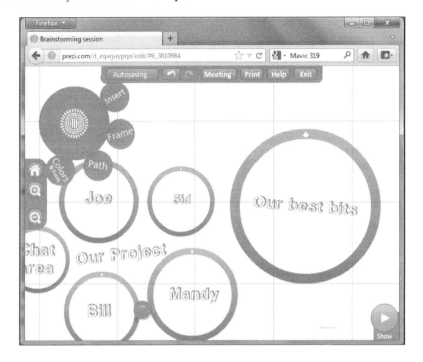

Keeping control

During an online presentation or collaboration, your guests have the opportunity to explore freely. They can do this by clicking on your avatar and then on **explore freely** in the speech bubble that appears:

If you're presenting something online, you'll need to keep an eye on who keeps exploring on their own. This might not be a bad thing as they could be looking at details in your presentation, but if you want to keep them focused ask them not to explore on their own just yet. If they ignore you and end up getting lost in the Prezi, just tell them to click on your name and then select the **Take a look** option. This will bring them all the way back to your location on the canvas.

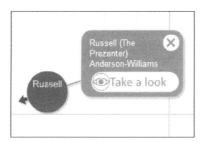

If you're allowing people to edit your Prezi, then exploring on their own is definitely a good thing. However, there will be times when you'll want everyone to be in one place. Just ask them to click on your name and then use the **Take a look** option. You can also use this option to follow any guest you want and see what they're working on.

If you set the Prezi meeting up, you will be the presenter. If you want to let someone else present to your group, just click their avatar and select **Hand Over Presentation**. This is a useful thing to do if subject matter experts want to talk to your audience.

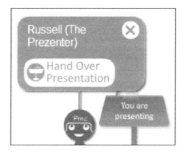

Removing access

If you're running a brainstorming session and have a number of people that can edit the Prezi, they will be able to log back in and make changes for up to one week. This might be okay if you want them to update it and then review the Prezi at the end of the week, but if you only want them to access it during the session you must remember to remove access once the session is finished.

Follow the given steps to remove access to your online Prezi:

1. Exit the Prezi canvas to go back to www.prezi.com.

2. Below the Prezi's preview window, click on the **Edit together** button.

3. To remove access for all, on the screen that appears, click the red **Reset share links** button.

4. To remove access for only certain individuals, click the cross to the right of their name. This is found under the **Who can edit** heading at the bottom of the screen.

Summary

A Prezi meeting can be a confusing place, so it's important to keep it simple and give good clear instructions. We'd recommend you keep all of the following points in mind in order to get the most out of this fantastic part of Prezi:

- Simple invite e-mail
- Good clear instructions
- Use of audio
- Practice time
- Freedom to explore
- Give directions to perform tasks and regroup

In the final chapter, we'll look at something that every Prezi user is bound to struggle with. Getting Prezi into your business is not easy, but there are a few ways in which you can try to win the hearts and minds of your colleagues.

11
Getting Prezi through the Door

We felt it wouldn't be right to finish this book without spending some time on the hardest task you're likely to face as a Prezi master. That task is getting Prezi through the door of your business, adopted, and loved by all your colleagues.

The very fact that you've purchased this book shows how much you appreciate Prezi. However, this isn't going to be the case for everyone in your business. With the constant grind of the day-to-day tasks it's difficult for workers to commit to learning new things. Prezi is not just a new piece of software but a whole new way of thinking and presenting.

To help you get Prezi through the door of your business we'll look at:

- PowerPoint's grip on business
- Opportunities to zoom
- Using PowerPoint to introduce Prezi
- Educating your business

PowerPoint's grip on business

Although we sing the praises of Prezis non-linear format and want everyone to be using it to create beautiful presentations, there's a lot to be said for a piece of software that's stuck around as long as PowerPoint has.

PowerPoint gave everyone in business the chance to be heard. Anybody could create a slideshow and make their message one hundred times louder than it was with just them saying the words. It added a visual element to important business messages, it was fairly easy to use, and has now become a standard piece of the kit that you expect to see in any organization. Credit where credit is due, those trusty old linear slides have helped most of us in business to create some decent enough presentations in our time.

But this is a different time, and the people joining today's workforce are very different thinkers to those from the good old days!

PowerPoint was created in a different decade, when people wore different types of suits to work, bread and milk were much cheaper, there was no Facebook or Twitter, companies didn't have to think outside the box that much to survive, and a presentation had to have beginning and end points. Ah, the good old days.

Nowadays companies will/should do all they can to look different than their competition, innovation is desperately sought after, and creativity is encouraged wherever possible. There's a constant wave of new organizations springing up shouting about how they think bigger and better than the next guys, and how innovative they are. How many of those companies' sales people have you let through the door to present to you, and then had to sit through a hundred tired old PowerPoint slides that have been passed down from one sales guy to the next. Innovative? Come on, really!

This is a perfect example of how tight a grip PowerPoint has on business presentations. We happily admit that it is a great tool, and it's changed the face of business presentations forever. But surely, it has to be time for a change, right? Unfortunately most people in business truly believe that PowerPoint is the only medium they have to present their ideas with, and until you show them otherwise the world's workforce will spend thousands of man hours each week sitting through slide after slide after slide. Zzzzzzzz!

The hard truth

Being a Prezi advocate as we're sure you are by now, the following news is going to be hard to deal with…

PowerPoint is going to be around in your business for a long, long time.

It would take some kind of miracle to introduce Prezi to your business on Monday, and have everyone hang up their PowerPoint boots by Friday to fully adopt Prezi as the new presentation tool of choice.

We really want to help you be as realistic as we think you should be. Yes your business may adopt Prezi, but we doubt very much that they'll totally ditch PowerPoint. If you can live with that fact then you'll save yourself a lot of stress and sleepless nights wondering why no one else gets it but you.

Fingers can remain crossed that in 25 years from now Prezi will be the number one presentation tool for business, but look at it this way: If some of your colleagues won't adopt Prezi and decide to stick with PowerPoint, whose presentations are going to have more impact?

Pssst, it's yours dummy!

The first hurdle

Before we look at some techniques to getting Prezi into your business we'll look at some of the questions you are bound to be asked when you first introduce it. Be ready for some very frosty stares from your colleagues!

- Why should I use Prezi?

    Because it will really help our presentations stand head and shoulders above competitors. Plus it has some really nifty features for helping us collaborate online and share ideas.

     A useful Prezi that explains why someone should use Prezi can be found at `http://prezi.com/jiie3wcg-qvx/ prezi-gives-content-bling/`.

- Can't I just import my PowerPoint slides?

    Yes you can, but we should then spend some time Prezifying them to get the most out of the software. Tell me the key points of Slide 2 and I'll show you how to zoom in and focus on them.

- It's just a fancier version of PowerPoint isn't it?

    Actually no, it's a completely different way of presenting that allows you to spread out your ideas on one canvas and see everything, rather than just move from slide to slide in one direction. PowerPoint imposes a hierarchy on your information, but Prezi allows you put your information into the hierarchy that suits you.

- I've seen a Prezi before and it made me feel sea sick!

    That's the fault of the presenter, not the software. We'll create your Prezi so that the audience feels engaged, not ill.

- Can I use animations and have things fading in and out and flying all over the place?

  Prezi doesn't have any animation features because it simply doesn't need them. The way you can move around the canvas is enough to grab your audience's attention.

- So I can only use Prezi online?

  Not at all. If we get you a Pro license you'll be able to use a desktop application and keep all your Prezis on your PC.

Opportunities to zoom

If by now you're trying to hatch plans that will see Prezi being used in your company then let us help you out. It's important you look for as many opportunities as possible to show off Prezi and get it in front of your colleagues so that they start to ask "Oooo how did you zoom in like that?"

You should be on the lookout for opportunities such as:

- Company events
- Training days
- Sales presentations

And it is also recommended that you start to build a list of colleagues that present as part of their job. They could be in sales, training, business development, or any other area of the business. Try to find out who hates presenting and tell them you can turn their slides into a rock concert that no one will forget!

Be prepared

An opportunity to show off Prezi could come along at any time. You need to be prepared to act fast so there's no time wasted at all. In *Chapter 9, Mastering the Newer Prezi Features*, we showed you how to brand your Prezis in order to make sure the corporate colors and logo were always present in your designs. With this in mind it's crucial that you create a branded Prezi template that can be used at any time. Your company is bound to have a standard PowerPoint template that people use, so create a company Prezi template and make sure it's always there when an opportunity arises.

Using the Theme Wizard

Follow these steps to create a standard company Prezi template:

1. Open the **Colors & Fonts | Theme Wizard**.

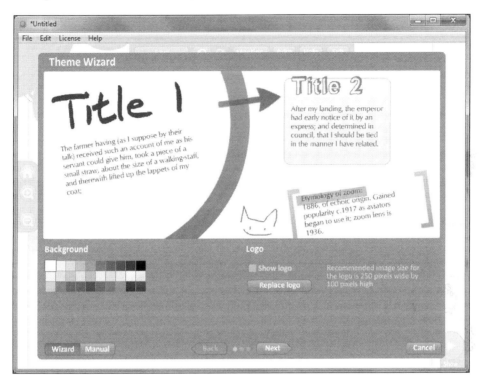

2. On the very first screen of the wizard, click on the **Replace Logo** button to add your company logo. The logo must be a .jpeg file, not larger than 250 pixels in width and 100 pixels in height. Clicking on this button will allow you to search for your logo and it will then be placed in the lower-left corner of your Prezi, every time.

3. On the next screen of the wizard we recommend you switch to the **Manual** mode by clicking on the option in the lower-left corner. In this screen you can select the fonts to use in your Prezi. At the present time Prezi still has only a limited number of fonts but we're confident you can find something close to the one your company uses.

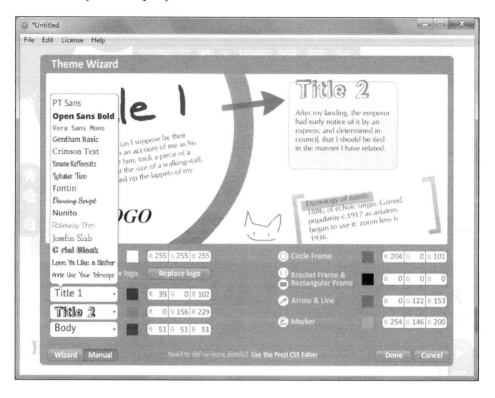

The reason we suggest switching to manual mode is because you'll be able to enter the RGB values for your corporate colors.

 You'll need to know the RGB color values specified in your corporate branding. If you don't know where to find them speak to a marketing person or someone in design. Definitely don't guess!

Frame templates

Way back in *Chapter 4, Approaching Your Prezi Design*, we explained that's it's a good idea to create frame templates that keep your Prezis style consistent. We'd definitely recommend you create these as part of your company Prezi template.

1. Go to a blank space on your canvas and place a frame there.

2. Enter some text inside the frame and call it templates so you don't forget what it's for.

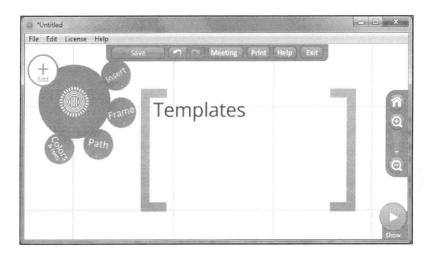

3. Inside this new frame create your frame templates to use throughout your Prezi. They can be as detailed or as simple as you like, and remember because Prezi zooms you will be able to place these templates inside one another in your design.

4. Use Prezi's rectangle shapes tool to indicate where images should be positioned, and simple text fields where information can be entered. The examples in the following screenshot, are very simple but hopefully give you the right idea:

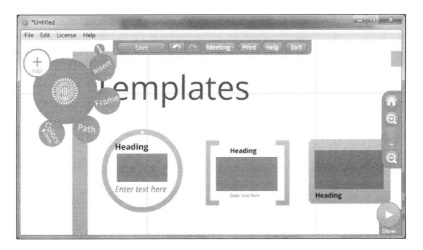

Once you have these frame templates in place, you can move to this area of your canvas at any time to copy one of them and then paste it into the position that is required in your design.

 Prezi's **+** button from the bubble menu will allow you to add frames and text together, but it is very limited and does not allow for customization of frames as described above.

Backing it up

Once you have your company's Prezi template, make sure you save it and back it up on a separate memory stick, or somewhere on the company server. When you're trying to win Prezi allies in your business this file will give you a huge advantage and enable you to act fast when you get the chance to Prezify a colleague's presentation for them. We'd also suggest you share this file and make its presence known to everyone in the business that has an interest in Prezi and builds presentations as part of their job.

Prezi Template
v0.1

Using PowerPoint to introduce Prezi

One of the best ways to win your colleagues over with Prezi is to fly under the radar and apply a very subtle approach. They'll all be used to seeing PowerPoint slides, so why not let them think that's what they're looking at and then WHAM! Hit them with a nice bit of Prezi zooming.

There's a couple of ways in which you can do this so we'll start with the simplest one first. Rest assured though that if you try this trick you are bound to have people asking about it after your presentation, and it's that level of curiosity that we really need to get us started.

Inserting PowerPoint slides

In *Chapter 7, Importing Slides into Prezi*, we saw how to insert PowerPoint slides into Prezi. A part of that chapter advised you to spread the slides out so they aren't as linear.

Slides being Prezified

If you're Prezifying some PowerPoint slides then we still recommend you spread the slides out. However, if you're trying to give Prezi a low profile so that it subtly grabs attention, insert your slides and line them up next to one another in a linear format.

"What, this is madness!", we hear you Prezi masters saying, but, trust us for a second. Follow these steps:

1. Insert your slides and line them up, as shown in the following screenshot:

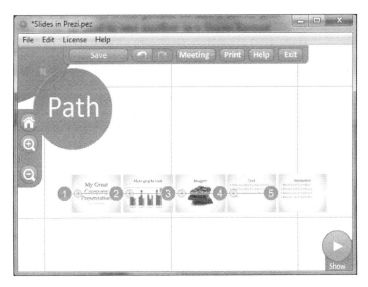

2. Link them together in order with a Path.

3. Insert frames around the key bits of information that will be talked about in the presentation:

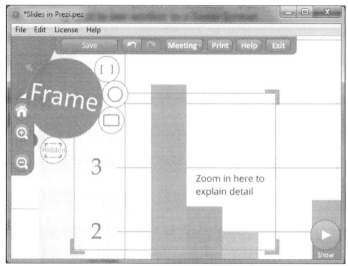

Graphs are perfect for zooming in on details

4. Link these key areas to your path so that you zoom into them during the presentation.

 When you use the zoom feature don't make a big deal out of it. Just casually carry on as if this way of presenting is completely normal.

What you'll end up with here is a presentation that looks and feels very much like PowerPoint. It is very linear in nature, but subtly introduces Prezi's abilities to zoom in on important details. We aren't going to worry about showing off the ability to enter YouTube clips, Prezi Meeting, and non-linear designs; we're just going to make people go, "Oh! I like that".

If you wanted to be a bit more obvious that you aren't using PowerPoint, you could also zoom out to show a full overview at the end of your presentation. You can see in the following screenshot, that we've zoomed out to show all our slides and to ask if there are any questions:

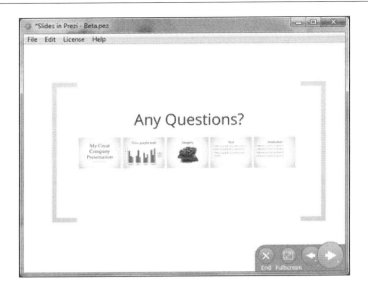

If your business isn't used to see Prezis then we guarantee the one question you will definitely get at this stage is "How did you make that presentation?". Once that question is asked you can start to introduce more of Prezi.

Building a PowerPoint presentation

From the heading above you're probably thinking, "They've finally gone mad. Over 200 hundred pages and now they want me to use PowerPoint!" Again please just go with us on this one. We promise it won't be a waste of time.

Let's take the same slides we saw just now. We already have them in PowerPoint so why don't we use that for our presentation, but insert a Prezi onto one of the slides to show off some zooming. The slide with the graph would again be the perfect candidate to do this with.

Slide Dynamic

There's a nice Prezi plugin for PowerPoint that's been developed by some clever people at a company called **Slide Dynamic**. It does come at a price but you can download the free trial at `http://www.slidedynamic.com/slidedynamic-addin/download-trial`.

This great little gizmo allows you to drop online or offline Prezis into your PowerPoint presentation really easily. What you end up with then is an old tired PowerPoint that people will initially roll their eyes at, injected with a fresh new way to engage your audience.

Before we show you how to use the plugin, grab yourself an old company PowerPoint and save a duplicate copy of it onto your PC. Select the slide you'd like to Prezify and delete all of the others. Save the remaining slide as a PDF file and insert it into Prezi.

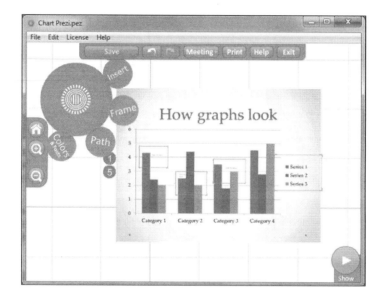

You can see in the preceding screenshot that we've inserted our slide containing the graph. Once in Prezi we've added frames and paths to zoom in on important details. Make sure you do a good job of Prezifying the slide you select.

Before you follow the steps mentioned in the following sections, make sure you've installed the Slide Dynamic trial from `http://www.slidedynamic.com/slidedynamic-addin/download-trial`. Once it is installed, you'll see the **SlideDynamic** tab at the top of your PowerPoint menu, as shown in the following screenshot:

The following sections show how to use the plugin.

Offline Prezis

To insert a Prezi that's been created in the Prezi desktop application follow these steps.

1. Click on **File** and select **Export as portable prezi...**.

2. Save the file in the same folder that your original PowerPoint presentation is being stored in:

3. Right click (*Ctrl* + click for Mac users) on the zipped folder containing your Prezi and select **Extract All** for extracting the files to the same location again.

4. Open the zipped folder and copy (*Ctrl C* or *command* + *C* for Mac users) all of the files contained within:

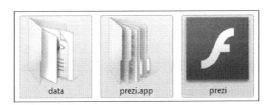

5. Paste (*Ctrl V* or *command* + *Y* for Mac users) the files back into the original location of your PowerPoint file:

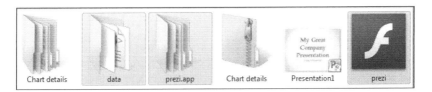

 What you should end up with is everything that your exportable Prezi needs, along with the original PowerPoint slides all in one folder.

6. Now open the PowerPoint file and go to the slide in which you'd like to insert your offline Prezi.

7. Click on the **Slide Dynamic** tab at the top of PowerPoint and select **Insert offline Prezi**:

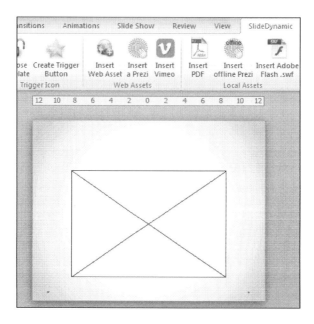

8. Drag the corners of the box that appears to resize your Prezi and fill the entire slide.

9. Go into presentation mode (*F5* or *Ctrl + Shift + S* for Mac users) to see the Prezi working inside your PowerPoint.

What you should end up with is a very obvious PowerPoint slide show with a little injection of Prezi thrown in.

Online Prezis

To insert an online Prezi is much simpler, but of course you need to have an Internet connection to get things to work.

1. Browse to the online Prezi you want to insert and copy the web URL from the top of your browser:

2. Open PowerPoint and locate the slide you'd like to insert your Prezi onto.

3. Click on the **Slide Dynamic** tab and then **Insert a Prezi**:

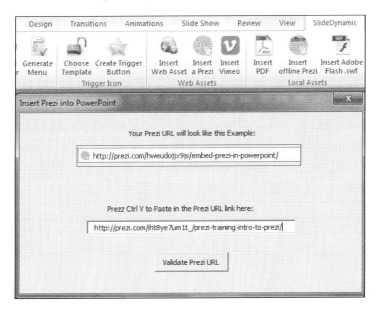

4. Paste the URL link into the field at the bottom of the screen that appears and click on **Validate Prezi URL**.

5. Once validated you can click on **Embed Prezi** and your Prezi will be available to view in presentation mode.

Again, what you'll end up with is a very subtle introduction to Prezi without distracting people too much from the linear format they are used to in PowerPoint.

Educating your business

A part of introducing Prezi to your business is going to be educating them. It includes showing your colleagues how to use it, and also how to think and approach designs in the right way.

You'll be happy to know that the Prezi website does have a large amount of useful information on its Learn pages (`http://prezi.com/learn`). As, you can see in the following screenshot, there are some videos available from the Prezi site which you can point colleagues to:

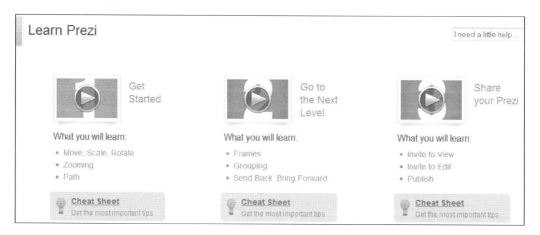

 You can also ask for the help of an official Prezi expert at http://prezi.com/experts/.

Company's how-to guide

It's highly recommended that before you start getting people excited about Prezi you prepare a very simple "How-to" document that uses some of the basic instructions from the site. The best place to source some useful information is `http://prezi.com/learn/manual` which contains lots of useful info on all of Prezi's features.

Manual				Back to Learn Cen
Getting started	Editing your prezi	Presenting & Managing	Knowledge Base	**Support**
How can I get prezi?	**The Prezi environment**	**Present**	Frequently Asked Questions	Report a problem to get help from the Prezi staff and community
Choosing your Prezi licence Plan: FAQ	Known Issues	Download a Portable Prezi for presenting	Support	Twitter Support
Alternate way to get an EDU email address	Prezi zoomed away	Print a prezi	New Feature Log	Known Issues
How to: upgrade, cancel account, handle unsuccessful payments	Prezi Editor	Present from a browser	System Requirements	Prezi zoomed away how to restore it
	Edit Mode / Show Mode	Plugging into a projector		
	Bubble Menu	Smart Zooming		
Cancellation and	Keyboard shortcuts	Remote clicker		
	Navigation	Auto Play Prezi		

Once you have a big group of colleagues who all want to know more about Prezi, you can hand them this book. See, it was totally worth the investment!

Summary

Hopefully you've figured out by now that it's not just about getting Prezi through the door of your business. It's about slowly introducing its features, winning over the mindsets that have been so used to linear presentations, and more than anything, being fully prepared to create a Prezi at a moment's notice without stomping all over your company's branding guidelines. If you take the time to prepare now, you'll stand a much better chance of successfully introducing Prezi into your business.

In the next chapter, wait, there is no next chapter. Go forth and be a Prezi master. Good luck!

Index

D

death by Prezi 70
drawings and diagrams templates
  about 183-185
  locating 183
  selecting 183-185
DrawIt (Mac format only) 8
DrawPlust 8

E

Edit menu, WLMM 60
edit mode, Prezi viewers 155
Edu Enjoy license 46
effects, YouTube 55
embedded Prezis 122
enhancements, YouTube
  audio 55
  effects 55
  Quick Fixes menu 54
Enjoy license 46
explore freely option 208

F

F4V 45
FLV 46
font colours 188, 189
Frame templates 218, 219
free audio libraries
  URLs 30
From web feature 11
fun with video
  about 63
  customer scenarios 63
  information from experts 63
  quizzing 63

G

GIF (Graphics Interchange Format) 7
GIMP 6
Google image search
  advanced image search 13
  limitations 15
  standard search 14
  using 13

GrafX2 6
grouping and moving
  about 193
  frame, using 193
  Shift key, using 194

H

Hand Over Presentation option 209
highlighter tool 181
highlighting, online design approach
  color, used 124-126
  frames, used 123
Home menu, WLMM 58, 59

I

imagery
  about 5
  finding 10
  raster 5, 6
  right images, finding 10
  vector 5, 6
  vectorising 17-21
imagery, Prezi checklist
  about 145
  spell check 146
  text 146
  zoom 146
imagery types
  raster 9
  vector 10
Inkscape
  about 8
  downloading 18
  URL 18
insert from web function
  about 11
  limitations 12
Insert YouTube option, Prezi
  about 50
  right clip, searching 52
interactive Prezis
  about 106
  using 108, 109
  working 106, 107
Interactive Whiteboard (IWB) 106
invitation e-mail 202

Thank you for buying
Mastering Prezi for Business Presentations

About Packt Publishing

Packt, pronounced 'packed', published its first book "*Mastering phpMyAdmin for Effective MySQL Management*" in April 2004 and subsequently continued to specialize in publishing highly focused books on specific technologies and solutions.

Our books and publications share the experiences of your fellow IT professionals in adapting and customizing today's systems, applications, and frameworks. Our solution based books give you the knowledge and power to customize the software and technologies you're using to get the job done. Packt books are more specific and less general than the IT books you have seen in the past. Our unique business model allows us to bring you more focused information, giving you more of what you need to know, and less of what you don't.

Packt is a modern, yet unique publishing company, which focuses on producing quality, cutting-edge books for communities of developers, administrators, and newbies alike. For more information, please visit our website: www.packtpub.com.

Writing for Packt

We welcome all inquiries from people who are interested in authoring. Book proposals should be sent to author@packtpub.com. If your book idea is still at an early stage and you would like to discuss it first before writing a formal book proposal, contact us; one of our commissioning editors will get in touch with you.

We're not just looking for published authors; if you have strong technical skills but no writing experience, our experienced editors can help you develop a writing career, or simply get some additional reward for your expertise.

Adobe Flash 11 Stage3D (Molehill) Game Programming Beginner's Guide

ISBN: 978-1-84969-168-0   Paperback: 412 pages

A step-by-step guide for creating stunning 3D games in Flash 11 Stage3D (Molehill) using AS3 and AGAL

1. The first book on Adobe's Flash 11 Stage3D, previously codenamed Molehill

2. Build hardware-accelerated 3D games with a blazingly fast frame rate.

3. Full of screenshots and ActionScript 3 source code, each chapter builds upon a real-world example game project step-by-step.

4. Light-hearted and informal, this book is your trusty sidekick on an epic quest to create your very own 3D Flash game.

Flash Game Development by Example

ISBN: 978-1-84969-090-4   Paperback: 328 pages

Build 9 classic Flash games and learn game development along the way

1. Build 10 classic games in Flash. Learn the essential skills for Flash game development.

2. Start developing games straight away. Build your first game in the first chapter.

3. Fun and fast paced. Ideal for readers with no Flash or game programming experience.Topic

4. The most popular games in the world are built in Flash.

Please check **www.PacktPub.com** for information on our titles

PUBLISHING

Flash Multiplayer
Virtual Worlds

Build immersive, full-featured interactive worlds for games, online communities, and more.

Makzan

Flash Multiplayer Virtual Worlds

ISBN: 978-1-84969-036-2   Paperback: 412 pages

Build immersive, full-featured interactive worlds for games, online communities, and more

1. Build virtual worlds in Flash and enhance them with avatars, non player characters, quests, and by adding social network community

2. Design, present, and integrate the quests to the virtual worlds

3. Create a whiteboard that every connected user can draw on

4. A practical guide filled with real-world examples of building virtual worlds

Quick answers to common problems

Flash Facebook
Cookbook

Over 60 recipes for integrating Flash applications with the Graph API and Facebook.

James Ford

Flash Facebook Cookbook

ISBN: 978-1-84969-072-0   Paperback: 388 pages

Over 60 recipes for integrating Flash applications with the Graph API and Facebook

1. Work with the key Graph API objects and their social connections, using the Facebook ActionScript 3 SDK.

2. Create new Checkins at Facebook Places and plot existing Checkins and Facebook Places on Flex mapping components.

3. Upload image files or generated images to Facebook.

4. Packed full of solutions using a recipe-based approach.

Please check **www.PacktPub.com** for information on our titles

Made in the USA
Lexington, KY
11 March 2014